ISBN 0-9653272-0-5

Library of Congress Catalog Card Number: 96-077334

Published by Gray Castle Press
3401-A167 Adams Avenue
San Diego, California 92116-2429

CONTRASTS

SHORT VERSION FOR BROADCASTS

JIMMY DORSEY
1933

# CONTENTS

# ILLUSTRATIONS

# PREFACE

Although this work is primarily about my becoming a professional musician and my experiences of traveling with a name "big band," in a larger sense I'd rather think of it as revealing anecdotes about Jimmy Dorsey and his orchestra that have never been brought to light. For some reason, to this day no one has written about this man and his music in any depth.

I hope this little opus sheds some light on an extremely complex, talented and fascinating musician, his devoted band of "crazies," and the twilight years of the big band era.

Perhaps, in reading this, the younger generation of musicians and music fans will come to appreciate the many fine players — most of whom are no longer with us — who were completely dedicated to their art. And, hopefully, although big bands are long-gone, the current crop of players will apply that same dedication to the furtherance of *good* music.

> Gene Bockey
> San Diego, California
> Spring, 1996

*For Eric and Dana*

# ACKNOWLEDGEMENT

I want to thank my good friend, fellow Horace Mann Junior High and San Diego High School classmate, and jazz aficionado Don Kader, for his countless hours of editing help.  After perusing my manuscript many times over, he corrected my errors in spelling, punctuation, and, of course, my jazzman's sometimes sinful syntax and grammar.  His indexing and computerization of this tome has resulted in a more mellifluous and readable format.

*G.B.*

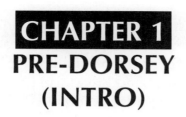

# CHAPTER 1
# PRE-DORSEY
# (INTRO)

I was born Eugene Dale Bockemuehl — a wonderful moniker for a classical composer, mid-town Manhattan doorman, or Nazi general — but not suitable for someone destined to be a big band and jazz musician. By my senior year in high school I had changed it to a more euphonious "Gene Bockey."

Unfortunately, I was born in 1925, ten years too late to become a successful big band leader. By 1955, television, "listening" bands such as Stan Kenton, pseudo-vocalists, Petrillo's two stupid recording bans and Rock (properly spelled C-R-A-P) had hit the fan. Musicality and ballroom dancing had all but disappeared, taking away the wonderful, danceable and harmonically-advanced bands and soloists of the '30s and '40s.

I originally became interested in music via inattention and mischief during "singing things" in kindergarten at Grant School in San Diego. My teacher, Mrs. Anderson, would say, "Eugene, come stand by the piano." Also, my mother's piano rendition of Gustav Lange's syrupy *Flower Song* (the only tune she could play), and my baby-sitter's version of the popular (1929) *Wedding of the Painted Doll* really blew my mind.

Later, I joined Grant School's fourth grade harmonica band. We had a socko arrangement of *I'm Heading for the Last Round-Up* which we eventually performed on the stage of San Diego's California Theater under the sponsorship of Wonder Bread.

I began playing clarinet at age nine in the 235-member "Bonham Brothers Greater San Diego Boys Band" led by Jules F. Jacques — a taskmaster. (The Bonhams were the premier funeral directors in San Diego, but they wanted to keep marching band music alive!) By age 12 I was playing alto saxophone, and rendering Rudy Wiedoeft solos with the band at San Diego's Ford Bowl, Russ Auditorium, Balboa Park Organ Pavilion and in local churches.

I studied privately with John Schreiber, a working musician with dance orchestras and pit bands. He was a stickler on technique, and taught me the secrets of playing dance music. We'd start each lesson with my playing all the major scales from memory.

During the '30s and '40s the Bonham organization was probably the best youth band in the United States. In the summers of 1935 and 1936 we performed at the California Pacific International Exposition in Balboa Park almost every day. In 1938 we took first place in the All-Western Band Review in Oakland, beating out a cocky band composed of older kids from Pine Bluff, Arkansas. In 1939 we were featured for a week, along with the Edwin Franko Goldman band (Sousa's successor) at the World's Fair in San Francisco. And I still cherish my four-time participation with the Bonham Band in Pasadena's New Year's Day Rose Parade.

In the '30s my parents rented a little house at 3955 Falcon Street in San Diego's Mission Hills district. I spent a lot of time in the attic where our landlady had stored a Victrola and several records. I played my clarinet along with the Vocalion and Brunswick discs, and got really "hot" on Abe Lyman's *Snake Hips* and Ted Lewis' *Down the Old Church Aisle*. When I was on parade with the Bonham Band (clarinets were in the rear), I usually ad libbed the Sousa marches since the leader couldn't hear me from that far back!

During the Great Depression, although my father, Fred Bockemuehl, worked 72 hours a week at his own clothes cleaners in Logan Heights, he always kept Sundays open and would take my mother, Emily, and me to matinees downtown at either the Fox or Orpheum Theaters (neither of which, unfortunately, still exist). The bills usually featured a film, a Movietone Newsreel, a cartoon, a short subject, and on-stage vaudeville including a famous name band (all for 35 cents!). These venues allowed me to see the bands of Duke Ellington, Paul Whiteman, Buddy Rodgers, Cab Calloway, Chico Marx and Ted Lewis.

I once saw Ginger Rogers lose her panties during a dance routine. I stayed for the next show, but, unfortunately, it didn't happen again.

My eyes and ears were really opened one night in 1940 when I stood in the front row to watch the Charlie Barnet Orchestra at Pacific Square Ballroom, San Diego's premier big band showcase. The next day I went to a hock shop and bought a straight soprano saxophone (like Charlie's) for 25 bucks!

My first "gig" was in 1940, a job in the Bill Thorpe orchestra at the Emerald Hills Country Club in south San Diego, with a bunch of much older guys. Since I was the best player (at age 15), they put me on lead alto. We had six "stock" arrangements, and played them over and over for the entire four-hour job. Even at that stage, I knew this was a crappy band.

At San Diego High, after a year of playing in teacher Russell Warren's school dance band, I organized my own group to play at "Teeners" every Saturday night at the VASA Club House on El Cajon Boulevard (it's still there — the VASA, not "Teeners"). We eventually were able to book many high school and college dances, as well as playing for free at Army and Navy USO functions around town.

A young sailor, Earle Spencer (I just remembered his name, after 54 years!), who was a devoted fan of Stanley Kenton's new band at the Rendezvous Ballroom in Balboa, California, started attending our rehearsals. He later began bringing in copies of arrangements Kenton was using at the Rendezvous. Soon, Kenton's charts of *Reed Rapture, Taboo, Tempo di Joe, Lamento Gitano, Deep River*, and *Jam Fever* were on our stands at the VASA Clubhouse. They all had that early monotonous Kenton trademark figure ( ♪ ♩ ♩ ♩ ♪ ).

Earle Spencer made it through the war, got out of the Navy, eventually organized a Kenton "copy-cat" band, and recorded some unsuccessful discs for Black & White Records.

I first saw the Jimmy Dorsey band at Pacific Square Ballroom in 1941 when I was 16 years old. When he appeared at the Mission Beach Ballroom, I borrowed arranger Marvin Wright's chart of *Alto-tude*, an original written for Jimmy. My lead trombonist, Dick Taylor, and I stayed up all night copying the parts so it would be back on the bandstand the following night. Henceforth, we used it for our theme song. From then on, I showed up in front of the bandstand at all of Dorsey's engagements in San Diego. At Pacific Square in 1944, a year after my graduation from San Diego High, Jimmy finally invited me up on the stand to play some choruses on a *Blues in B♭*. My friends

Bill Kraft and George Handy (who was writing for the Boyd Raeburn and Alvino Rey bands) were in the audience urging me on.

Jimmy had originally heard me on some home recordings when my style was a combination of Coleman Hawkins, Benny Carter and himself, but I had recently been exposed to Dizzy Gillespie and Charlie Parker. He was appreciative of my technique; my playing in the then-new "bebop" style surprised and interested him. Jimmy was all grins when I ended the evening by playing his theme song, *Contrasts*, just like him. Several boppers — Al Haig, Herb Ellis, Red Rodney and Serge Chaloff, were with the band — as well as potent performers Babe Russin and Conrad Gozzo. Jimmy's road manager, Gil Koerner, offered me a job, and almost in tears, I had to tell him that I was due to report to the U.S. Army in 19 days. Damn it! Damn it!!

During this period I was sitting in with various black musicians in San Diego's Logan Heights area at The Black and Tan Cafe, The Pickadilly Club and at former light-heavyweight boxing champion Archie Moore's Chicken Shack. I even played steady for a while, along with Bill Kraft, with Froebel "Fro" Brigham's black group at the Creole Palace in the Douglas Hotel on Market Street (the only black-owned hotel in town). I would often be in "cutting contests" with Harold Land and Kirk Bradford (Mustafa Hashim). I was a big favorite with the fly black chicks, but they scared me to death with their advances (after all, I was all of 18 years old!).

While soloing one night with some local cats at the Chicken Shack, I noticed that the string bass suddenly sounded a hell of a lot better than usual. Turning, I saw Eddie Safranski standing next to me. Shortly, Art Pepper, Bart Varsalona, Shelly Manne, Bob Cooper and June Christy were on the stand. Suddenly I realized that Stan Kenton's entire band was in the room — what a gas!

Art thoroughly cut me to ribbons — but not for long.

**The "Not Quite Ready for Big Bands" Altoist (1937)**

### THE PLEDGE REQUIRED OF EACH BONHAM

**BAND BOY** is a guarantee that he is a young gentlemen, that he is a patriotic citizen, and that he is living a clean and vigorous life. Those are the principles upon which the Bonham Brothers Boys Bands of San Diego, California, are built. The able bandmaster is Jules Jaques (inset). The senior band is composed of 100 pieces and the junior band includes 115 pieces. The bands use 97 Conn instruments.

**(1935)**

To My good friend
Gene Bockemuehl.
Here's hoping to see you
in Civies soon — and —
leading a wonderful Band —
You deserve it —
Sincerely
Jimmy Dorsey

**JIMMY DORSEY**
And his Orchestra

MANAGEMENT
**GENERAL AMUSEMENT CORP.**
NEW YORK · CHICAGO · HOLLYWOOD · CINCINNATI · LONDON

**"Teeners"**
**Vasa Clubhouse**
**1942**

Front Row:
      Frank Rose
      Gene Bockey
      Ray Peabody
      Rube Goldstone
      *Manuel Morante

Second Row:
      Jack Trott
      Harry Hubbard
      Dick Taylor
      Creed Brawner
      Louis Smith

**Gene Bockemuehl**
**Orchestra**

Leader - $3.00 - 4 Hrs.
Sidemen - $2.50 - 4Hrs
* - Unpaid

* Ruby Harding (singer)

# CHAPTER 2
## BORRACHO EN TIJUANA

Upon reporting for active duty as a puny, 115-pound musician, the United States Army, in it's infinite wisdom, molded me into a ferocious infantry rifleman. After strolling through France, Luxembourg and Belgium (into a little rest stop called "The Bulge"), I was wounded in Der Vaterland (thank God — you could get killed out there!), and spent the last nine months of my soldiering career in six different GI hospitals.

Back home in early 1946, I waltzed (exaggerating my slight limp) into Pacific Square Ballroom to see Jimmy Dorsey. I was carrying a brand-new French Selmer alto saxophone that had set me back 385 hard-earned dollars. When I showed it to Jimmy he said, "Holy Christ, why did you do that? The Selmer Company sends me a new one every year, and I'd have given you one. I hate to see the damn Frogs making money off Americans!"

I sat in with the band again, and after the job Dorsey asked my date Helen Rister and me to go to Tijuana, Mexico with him. Helen said, "I'll have to ask my father," and I said, "I've got to get my dad's car (a 1928 Model "A" Ford) back home so he can drive it to work tomorrow." (We also had a 1941 Chevrolet Special Deluxe Club Coupe — I still have it — but it was a "Sunday only" vehicle then.)

Dorsey and "The Champ" (Al Joslow, Jimmy's valet/bodyguard) followed me home to Mission Hills in Jimmy's Buick Roadmaster station wagon. We then progressed to Helen's house in the newly-developed subdivision of Linda Vista. Dorsey, who was already feeling no pain, barged into Helen's parents' bedroom and said to her father, "My name is Jimmy Dorsey. I can tell by your red hair that you're a goddamned Irishman like myself. I'm taking your daughter and her boyfriend to Tijuana tonight. There will be no hanky-panky. Okay?" Helen's father mumbled, "Okay," and her mother just sat up in bed and stared. We were on our way.

As we rolled south through National City, Dorsey asked if we didn't think it was rather presumptuous of the founding fathers to give that wide spot in the road such a high-sounding name. Then the subject of birthdays came up. Jimmy was a leap year baby — February 29th; Helen and I were both born on February 20th. Jimmy laughingly said, "You two should never fool around because that could be construed as incest!"

We hit just about every nightclub on Avenida Revolucion, Tijuana's main drag, sucking up mucho booze, and Dorsey insisted that I sit in with every Ranchero and Mariachi band. We had huevos rancheros and tequila for breakfast at 9 a.m., and took Helen home.

From there, The Champ wheeled the Roadmaster onto Highway 101 and headed for Los Angeles. Dorsey said, "I can't mess around here any longer. You're coming home with me. My clothes will fit you, I'll get you a toothbrush, and you can 'phone your folks when we get to my place."

**Helen Rister**

# CHAPTER 3
# A WEEK AT THE DORSEY PAD

Jimmy's 12-room Tudor mansion was situated in the Toluca Lake area of North Hollywood. Bob Hope, Bing Crosby, and a doctor, who administered vitamin B12 shots to sober up his buddies, were his immediate neighbors. Jimmy's wife, Jane (Miss Detroit of 1925) and their 17-year-old daughter, Julie Lou, were in residence. An old "colored" couple, Ben (an ex-hoofer) and Victoria Murphy, served as butler and cook/housekeeper. They lived in an apartment over the garage.

The home was originally built for movie stars Dick Powell and Joan Blondell. It had a large pool, an adjoining game room equipped with a motion picture projector and screen, two tennis courts and a haven for doves and pigeons. The back gate opened onto the third tee of the Lakeside Country Club. Jimmy always referred to his home as "nice little place with a golf course."

That first afternoon, after I had called home, Jimmy and I drank and listened to recordings and transcriptions of what he considered his better bands. I liked the five-trumpet 1944 band the best. Dorsey ended the session with a recording of his favorite classical piece: Delius' *On Hearing the First Cuckoo in Spring*, a beautiful coda to the day. He really loved that composition — it brought back happy memories of his friendship with Bix Beiderbecke during the Paul Whiteman days.

After many more "shooters" and very little dinner, we were off to Club 47 in the San Fernando Valley. Jimmy insisted that I sit in with Eddie Miller's fine Dixieland group. Hell, I can play Dixie, but Dorsey wanted me to play bop. The band wasn't too thrilled, and neither was I. Also, I was uncomfortable playing a strange horn — Jimmy's. Sometimes, life is just a bowl of weevils!

From there we went to guitarist Nappy Lamare's home in Hollywood. Jimmy tried to talk Nappy into going back on the road with him when the band reorganized, but Lamare wanted to stay in town with his family. Dorsey finally gave up, but insisted that Nappy wake up his three little boys so I could play bebop for them — this time "a cappella." When they trooped in, I was too embarrassed and stubborn to play. Dorsey was quite miffed. He told me that I owed it to the kids to play. NUTS!

Our last stop was Ben Pollack's rib joint on the Sunset Strip. Pollack, a fine drummer, led a very popular jazz-oriented big band in the late '20s and early '30s. He was a remarkable talent scout, and had discovered Harry James, Irving Fazola, Jack Teagarden, Glenn Miller, Nappy Lamare, Eddie Miller, Charlie Spivak, Ray Bauduc,

Benny Goodman, Matty Matlock and Yank Lawson. (Jack Teagarden should have eventually taken over Pollack's band, but he wasn't available. A non-musician, Bob Crosby, ended up waving a long baton — out of meter — in front of that very good jazz aggregation.)

Anyway, I ended up sitting in with Pollack that night. Just his drums and my alto sax — what a group — but he sure kept good time!

While we were there, a middle-aged "nymphet" taloned Dorsey, and he said to me, "I'm gonna get my cack sacked, so I'll drop you off at the house." Hell, I was happy to finally get to bed! Ben Murphy put me in Jimmy's bedroom, which was gigantic. Dorsey's two huge steamer trunks in the middle of the room looked insignificant. You could have put my folks' living and dining rooms, plus the kitchen, in that space! Jane had her own bedroom.

Jimmy rolled in at 7 a.m. and informed me that we had a golf date in an hour at the Lakeside course. Shit, I'd never played in my life, but said I'd walk around with him.

The foursome ended up being Bob Hope, the film comedienne Cass Daley, her husband, and Dorsey. I tagged along with the caddy, and he cautioned me not to make a shadow when they were putting. Hope kept trying to talk Jimmy into appearing on his weekly radio show, but Dorsey said it was necessary that he take the band back on the road. They had been stagnant on the West Coast too long while filming *"The Fabulous Dorseys."* So instead, Hope hired Les Brown — and you know the rest of the story!

Jimmy, still half-loaded and into his third day without sleep, managed to shoot a respectable 83 for the round. Both Jimmy and brother Tommy could go days without sleep. Irish cats are something else!

Afterwards, we repaired to the Daley home for cocktails — what else!

Subsequently, we managed to float down to Studio City for dinner at the Sportsman's Lodge on Ventura Boulevard, one of the "in" restaurants at the time. You were expected to catch your own trout in a stream in back of the joint and have the chef cook it for you. We had spaghetti. Midway through the meal, Dorsey passed out in his plate of pasta — a three-point landing! Cass simply said, "Oh, the dear man is just tired," and went on with her dinner. We eventually got Jimmy into the Dorsey (actually, Jane's} Cadillac, and I drove home. Ben helped me pour Jimmy into bed.

Both Jimmy and Tommy were stuck in Southern California during the filming of *"The Fabulous Dorseys."* Jimmy told me that in the bar scene with the brothers, Art

Tatum, Ziggy Elman and Charlie Barnet involved in a jam session, he personally filled the "movie drinks" with real booze, making Tommy mad as hell.

During the filming of the movie, the Dorseys had a massed-band "happening" at their Casino Gardens Ballroom in Santa Monica. Tommy, Jimmy and Harry James bought the place because Tommy was angry (he was always angry) with the owners of the Hollywood Palladium, and vowed to never play there again. The brothers had some special arrangements written, and it was a gas to hear Charlie Shavers soaring above a 15-piece brass section.

Tommy Rockwell, president of General Artists Corporation (GAC), personally came out to the house the next afternoon to plot the band's impending road trip. Rockwell tried to talk Dorsey into cutting down the size of the band for monetary reasons, but Jimmy indignantly shouted, "Don't you ever touch my band!"

Later, Al "The Champ" Joslow, came by to beg off the tour. Jimmy and he had a heated argument for about 15 minutes, but Dorsey finally submitted to Joslow's recommendation of Al Romano for a replacement as Jimmy's "gofer" and bodyguard.

I was hired to join the band when it was reorganized in New York. My starting salary would be $125 a week. At that time, my father was earning $60 a week as a foreman at Consolidated Aircraft Corporation in San Diego!

The entire Dorsey orchestra came over to Jimmy's mansion for hors d'oeuvres and cocktails one evening after playing at the Musicians Local 47's picnic. We all got smashed, and all I remember is talking to lead altoist Doc Rando and the vocalist, Dee Parker. Jimmy proudly showed everyone his soprano saxophone lamp, and Jane revealed all the secret hiding places Dick Powell had built into the house.

During the days Dorsey was busy at the movie studio, daughter Julie, her girl friend and I would play hearts and go swimming. Jane would often conspire with me to go to the kitchen and make her an orange juice and gin drink. I was in the middle because Julie asked me not to sneak drinks to her mother. One night, Jimmy and Jane, both more than half-gassed, tried to talk me into dating their daughter. They didn't care for the garage mechanic she was going with. I didn't endear myself to them by declining.

Jimmy cornered me one morning and said, "I put a few dents in Jane's Cadillac last night. While I'm at the studio, I want you and Ben to sneak it over to a garage on Lankershiem Boulevard and have them touch it up." Ben was frightened during the whole caper. I couldn't convince him that I was capable of driving the monster.

One evening, Dorsey informed Jane, Julie, Ben, Victoria and me that we were all going to the "wrap" party at the studio to celebrate the completion of *The Fabulous Dorseys."* I put on one of Jimmy's suits and was sitting on the bed contemplating meeting William Lundigan, Janet Blair, Paul Whiteman, Charlie Barnet and the other cast members, when a dolled-up Jane came in. She informed me that she and Jimmy had just had one hell of a spat, and he had departed in a huff. Jane apologized, and added, "... in spite of our argument, he should have at least taken you!"

Later, in 1950, I found a rare, 12-inch 78 rpm recording of Jimmy and Tommy playing the film's *Dorsey Concerto*, accompanied by the Cincinnati Symphony Orchestra under the direction of Fabian Sevitsky. Unfortunately, some non-musical asshole managed to sit on it!

Sic transit gloria movies!

Oddly, Jimmy Dorsey had hired me without actually knowing if I could read music. I had never sat in with the band's saxophone section. After a week at the Dorsey pad, and not wanting to wear out my welcome, I returned to San Diego to await my departure for New York.

**LOCAL BOY TO PLAY WITH JIMMY DORSEY'S ORCHESTRA**

Eugene Brockemuehl, son of Mr. and Mrs. F.W. Bockemuehl, 724 Sutter st., left Saturday for Hollywood, where he signed a contract to play the saxophone and clarinet with Jimmy Dorsey's orchestra.

The Group left Sunday for the east coast and will open their first engagement in Boston Oct. 14. They plan to return to the west coast in May.

When Jimmy Dorsey trekked east earlier this month, he took only key men intending to fill the band in New York for his east coast one-niter tour.

...Jimmy Dorsey and Columbia records were still negotiating at press time...

# CHAPTER 4
# MODULATING TO THE BIG APPLE

I had been attending San Diego State College on the GI Bill under Public Law 16 (for disabled veterans). Helen Rister finagled an excuse from a chiropractor friend (nervous exhaustion due to the late, great war), and I was able to obtain a leave of absence from the on-campus Veterans Administration representative.

Jimmy took a few of us from California, and the rest of the band was hired from Local 802 in New York City. Artie Lyons, first tenor sax, clarinet and copyist; Charlie Teagarden, second trumpet and vocals; Ray Bauduc, drums; and Howard Gibeling, arranger, were flown to New York.

Gil Koerner, road manager; his wife, Lila, secretary; Larry Noble, male vocalist; Brad Gowans, second valve/slide trombone; Maggie, Brad's very young girlfriend; and myself, second alto sax and clarinet, were delegated to drive the Buick Roadmaster station wagon to the east coast. God, it was so damned crowded carrying six people, the luggage and our instruments — how we managed to fit all of us and the gear in, I'll never know!

We all met at Gil and Lila's apartment in Long Beach, and left for New York around noon. We took turns driving the over-loaded monster, and very late the first night checked into a motel somewhere in the middle of the desert — our only goddamned stop-over for the entire trip!

Late the second night (morning!!!), we were in a traffic circle, I believe in Dallas, when a back door inadvertently opened and Gowan's quart bottle of Benzedrine tablets fell out and shattered on the pavement. We came to a screeching halt, and all of us spent quite a lot of time crawling all over the highway picking up bennies. I think that every other tablet Brad picked up went into his mouth. What a sight that must have been to passing motorists!

When we clambered back into the car, Brad informed us that he would assume all the driving chores from then on, and would go straight through to New York. I got in the front seat with him, determined to keep him awake. (Hell, come to think of it, the bennies did that!). The others got in back and went to sleep.

All the way across the country, Gowans sang Scottish ballads and lectured me about "the roots of jazz." One very lengthy and mile-consuming pontification concerned Bobby Hackett's complete mastery of chord structure and sequence.

We only stopped to eat; once we halted on a Sunday so Lila and Gil could attend Mass.

**My Home**

16

# CHAPTER 5
## MANHATTAN TRANSFER

Early one Fall morning, after a scary night of driving through the mountains of Virginia, we miraculously wound up on the Pulaski Skyway in New Jersey; the Manhattan skyline could be seen in the distance. We eventually pulled up in front of the Forrest Hotel (49th Street, west of Broadway, New York 19, N.Y.), OUR HOME, and checked in.

I was assigned to room with Ray Bauduc. At that time, single rooms were $2 a night (honest), and doubles were $3, so band members usually doubled up. I'll bet those same rooms go for over $100 a night today (if the hotel is still standing). Ray was a little old lady. He'd wash his underwear in the sink, paste them and his hankies on the dresser mirror (so they'd be pressed when they dried), and put his trousers under the mattress before retiring so that the pleats would be creased in the morning. However, the only really annoying thing about rooming with Ray was the late-night visits by his innumerable friends. I distinctly remember the "John Barrymore of the Tenor Saxophone," Bud Freeman, bending my ear with musician stories from 2 a.m. until 6 one morning.

On my first night in the "Big Apple," San Diego buddies Bill Kraft (enrolled at Columbia University) and Don Beam ( who worked in the mail room of some company) came to the hotel bearing a gift of marijuana. I told them, "I can't jeopardize my career with this BIG-NAME-BAND by smoking grass." Of course, in my youthful naivete I didn't know then that half the Dorsey band were "gage heads," and all of them were dedicated  boozers!

My initial experience with a New Yorker occurred when I gave a salesperson five cents for a pale yellow "orange drink" at Nedick's. She actually bit the nickel to see if it was legitimate. No Californian will believe this — but it's a fact!

You could get any kind of eats in Manhattan. Anything! The Mexican, Jewish and Chinese food, the pizza and cheese cake were the best I've ever eaten — even to this day. One could eat at the Automat for 20 cents, but cabbies and bellhops demanded a quarter tip.

A person didn't stroll and window shop along Broadway, but had to merge and march with the crowd to one's destination. However, once you got to the top of the Empire State Building, the view was unbelievable!

In the '40s the Manhattan skyline was still dominated by structures of style and grace, such as the Empire State, Woolworth and Chrysler buildings. Most large skyscrapers built since are uniformly ugly glass and steel rectangles. I'm sure King Kong would never deign to fight off airplanes from atop the U.N. Building or the World Trade Center!

And then there was baseball. My God, there were three major league baseball teams in New York! On off days/nights we would sometimes see Tommy Heinrich, Jerry Coleman (now the Malaprop radio/tv "voice" of the San Diego Padres), Phil Rizzuto, Hank Bauer, Joe DiMaggio, Yogi Berra, Eddie Lopat, Vic Raschi and Allie Reynolds go through their paces at Yankee Stadium. The great Casey Stengel was their manager.

Other times we'd go to Ebbets Field (an experience in itself) in Brooklyn. Dodgers Duke Snider, Pee Wee Reese, Carl Furillo, Gil Hodges, Roy Campanella, Jackie Robinson (his second year of being the first black in the major leagues), Carl Erskine, Preacher Roe and Billy Cox made history as "dem bums."

The Giants lineup at the Polo Grounds included such Hall-of-Fame names as Johnny Mize, Walker Cooper, Mel Ott and Bobby Thompson. Leo "The Lip" Durocher managed the team.

(All of this seemingly strange preoccupation with baseball stems from the fact that my father had once been a minor league pitcher in the "M.I.N.K" League (Minnesota, Iowa, Nebraska, Kansas). He would keep "slippery elm" in one cheek and tobacco in the other, and would overtly mix them on the "spit ball" before each pitch. He had a very successful record. Since I had small hands, he was grooming me to be a shortstop — until I got my first clarinet. His heart was broken until I began soloing with the Bonham Band.)

The first week in New York, Gil Koerner rehearsed the new band eight hours a day at Nola's Studios in Times Square. (Dizzy Gillespie was breaking in a new big band in the rehearsal studio next to us.) By the third day my lower lip was bleeding because of the rigorous schedule.

Gil had hired Dick Hoffman, lead trumpet; Joe Graves, third; Max Gussack, fourth; Doc Clifford, lead alto saxophone and clarinet; Phil Cenicola, second tenor, clarinet and flute; Mimi La Rocca, baritone sax, clarinet and bass clarinet; George Masso, lead trombone; Herb Winfield, Jr., third trombone and assistant conductor; Bill Lolatte, string bass; Alvin Waslohn, piano and arranger; Helen Lee, girl vocalist; and Gibby Seaborn, band boy. Gil had "liberated" many of them from the Ina Ray Hutton and Les and Larry Elgart orchestras, both of which were very good bands at the time. Jimmy and Al Romano were due to arrive at the end of the week.

A tailor came up to Nola's Studios the first week and during rehearsal breaks measured us for uniforms. We were outfitted with both dark blue and powder blue suits, and a checked sport coat. We wore maroon knit ties, white shirts and black shoes. "Mother" Bauduc taught me how to cut out a small piece of cardboard to wrap my breast pocket hanky around so I would always have a sharp, square, half-inch edge of white showing above the pocket.

Soon after the band was organized, Hoffman's wife gave birth to twins. Thereafter, on every payday, Lila would ask Dick, "How are the two twins?" Because of her sparkling personality, immense intellect and habit of always wearing the same ratty coat, Dick nicknamed her "The Couch." We also called her "Old Worms" because of her stunning beauty.

I had breakfast at the Times Square Schraft's restaurant (35 cents), and arrived at the first rehearsal very early and very nervous. My only experience with a professional big band had been a brief sojourn with Jack Teagarden's ill-fated and terrible 1946 congregation.

Although I was way too early, Gowans was already there. He had a handful of loose teeth, and was heating a stick of sealing wax. In awe, I watched him as he meticulously glued each tooth into his mouth. He had on a Boston Red Sox baseball cap, which he wore on all of our engagements.

Midway through the week Doc and Artie took me under their wings, steered me to a music store, and informed me that I needed to purchase a Brillhart 3-Star Mouthpiece in order to blend in better with the rest of the saxophone section. Although my reading had been fine, I knew that I had been just getting by with my "sound" on section work.

Also, I had almost run out of money. I was reticent about consulting any of these relative strangers, but was beginning to worry about room rent and meals. Obviously, I was very naive, and way over my head with this organization. In desperation, I finally went to Koerner. Gil said, "Hell, Gene, how much do you need? I thought you knew that you could draw on your first week's salary." He handed me a 50-dollar bill and sauntered away. Shoot, that was easy — it opened a whole new world for me!

One evening I found my way to Fifty Second Street where jazz proliferated in dozens of small clubs. The multitude of great, modern jazz groups just about blew me away, and way down the street I found old Sidney Bechet holding forth on his sopra-no saxophone. He was working in a crummy, beer-smelly upholstered sewer of a club with a lousy band, but his authentic New Orleans renditions with a "wider-than-a-barn" vibrato made hairs on my arms and back of my neck stand up — I still can't explain it! It wasn't my kind of music, but it was wonderful.

At the end of the week a sober and sun-tanned Dorsey arrived to rehearse and eval-uate the group Koerner had amassed. (Both Jimmy's synthetic tan and his sobriety were gone in a couple of weeks.) The first tune Jimmy called up was a written-out head arrangement entitled *Sneaky Pete*, which we hadn't previously rehearsed. He said, "Gene will take the alto solo." With that pronouncement, I was sure the band members were surprised and shocked, since Dorsey was a world-famous alto saxo-phonist, and I was an unknown West Coast piece of shit! To my knowledge, I'm the only alto player, other than himself, that Jimmy ever featured.

After that tune, I was finally accepted by the haughty New York cats, and especial-ly by Artie Lyons, whom I thought had been a little miffed and jealous because I had been given his second alto chair while he had been switched to tenor sax.

Doc Clifford "adopted" me and nicknamed me "The Eagle" because he said my playing reminded him of "The Bird," Charlie Parker. From then on, I was never called "Gene" again — except by Jimmy, Lila and Gil. Bill Lolatte even shortened my sobri-quet to "Eag."

Dorsey was unhappy with Gil's choice of the fourth trumpet player. Dick Hoffman and Joe Graves kept raving about, and bugging Jimmy to hire, an unknown teen-aged phenomenon from Canada, who supposedly possessed a fantastic high register. They had heard him when he played a couple of weeks with Boyd Raeburn's band. Anyhow, Max Gussack soon departed, and was replaced by 19-year-old Maynard Ferguson. After a few months, Helen Lee was replaced by Clare Hogan, Johnny Bothwell's ex-wife and vocalist. We picked her up in Canton, Ohio. Dorsey immedi-ately nicknamed her "Shanty" — notwithstanding the fact that the Dorsey clan wasn't exactly classified as "Lace-Curtain" Irish!

We broke in the band at the legendary Arcadia Ballroom on the night of that famous Broadway landmark's 24th anniversary. Dorsey had been a member of the Ray Miller band the night the dance palace opened. I got to solo on *Sneaky Pete*, and another clas-sic head-arrangement called *Oh Homer, Toss Me a Clam*. For a "sign-off" (to let the dancers know the set was over) we used the last two measures of the Dorsey Brothers 1934 arrangement of *By Heck*. My old high school buddies Bill Kraft and Don Beam were in the audience to witness my debut into the "big time!"

Dorsey also featured a Dixie contingent showcasing Charlie, Brad (later Herb Winfield), Artie on tenor and Jimmy on clarinet. It was known as "The Original Dorseyland Band." The approximating of both modern and traditional jazz was never a problem.

We didn't form separate, back-biting "cliques" within the band. Everyone got along famously. The library also included great arrangements by Toots Camarata, Joe Lipman, Sonny Burke, Harold Mooney, Don Redman, Freddy Slack and Marvin Wright. For a while, Dorsey even traded arrangements with the eccentric English orchestra leader, Ambrose.

I often asked Jimmy to dig out a strange "symphonic-style" 1940 arrangement of *High on a Windy Hill*, but he always said we'd have to rehearse it first. We never did.

My good friend Jack Trott and I always loved that chart, but never knew who arranged it. I thought it had to be either Joe Lipman or Tutti Camarata. Jack wrote to "Toots" in 1986, and got this answer:

*Dear John,*

*I received your letter re High on a Windy Hill. Your search is over — I am the culprit!*

*I particularly remember this arrangement as the band was working the Meadowbrook in Cedar Grove, N.J. when I brought it in to rehearsal.*

*Needless to say, I took plenty of ribbing both from Jimmy and the band .... why didn't I take it to the symphony?, etc.*

*Also, on the way out Rudy the bartender got on to me .... was I nuts?, etc...*

*The harmonic structure seemed to throw them, as it was written in E and F simultaneously.*

*I'm flattered you took the time to find out and hope this answers your question.*

*Regards,*
*Tutti"*

The doors have closed forever at Manhatten's last Automat

...Jimmy Dorsey and his crew will play during January at the Deshler-Wallick hotel in Colombus, Ohio.

RESTAURANTS
## Requiem for Horn & Hardart

The final jingle of change through the slot above the lion-head spout served a cup of coffee for eternity. Last week Horn & Hardart closed the nation's last surviving Automat, on New York City's 42nd Street, two blocks east of Grand Central station. First opened in 1912, the cafeterias served 400,000 customers a day at their peak in the early 1950s. Famous actresses, well-heeled businessmen and just plain folks plunked their coins into glass-and-chrome dispensers to feast on such fare as Boston baked beans, macaroni and cheese and coconut-custard pie.

In recent years, Automats fell victim to consumers' changing tastes. A generation weaned on fast-food outlets didn't see the point of all the fancy fixtures and the diverse menu. Nor did the upscale power lunchers have any use for the Automats' simple fare. "Those who've become successful stopped coming," says Michael Sherman, an executive vice president at Horn & Hardart, which is now concentrating on direct-mail catalogs. "They've been calling to ask why it's closing. I ask them, 'When was the last time you were there?' " ■

## JD Arcadia Date Brings Up Memories

New York — The Arcadia ballroom, Broadway landmark, celebrated its 24th anniversary with the debut of Jimmy Dorsey's new orchestra, which started an eastern tour of one-niters with this date. Jimmy used a nucleus of west coast men to build the new outfit.

The lineup has Doc Clifford, Gene Bockey, alto saxes; Phil Cenicola, Artie Lyons, tenors; Mimi La Rocca, baritone; Dick Hoffman, Charlie Teagarden, Joe Graves, Max Gussack, trumpets; George Masso, Herb Winfield, Brad Gowans, trombones; Ray Bauduc, drums; Johnny Jordan, guitar; Bill Lalotte, bass; Al Waslohn, piano, and Helen Lee, last with Larry Clinton, and Larry Noble, vocals.

Gathered at the anniversary celebration were many figures of the music world who attended the opening night festivities almost a quarter of a century ago.

On that first opening night, the bands of Ray Miller and Harry Reser were the featured attractions.

It is interesting to note that, just after finishing its Arcadia engagement, the Miller band took on a young saxophonist by the name of Jimmy Dorsey.

The Miller band that played the Broadway spot for its original opening had Ruby Bloom and Bill Fazzoli, pianos; Andy Sannella, Frank Trumbauer, Dick Johnson and Larry Abbott, saxophones; Charlie Rocco and Roy Johnson, trumpets; Ward Archer, drums; Frank De Prima, banjo; Pierre Oker, tuba; Danny Yates, violin; Tom Satterfield, arranger.

Reser had a banjo band with a lad named Red Nichols on trumpet.

## BY HECK SIGN-OFF

# CHAPTER 6
# ONE-NIGHTERS IN NEW ENGLAND

Our first one-nighter was at the Armory in North Adams, Massachusetts. Charlie and Ray's wives (Florence and Edna) had arrived in New York to ride the band bus with us, so I began rooming with Brad. It was Fall, and being a thin-blooded Southern Californian, I damn near froze my gizzard (and other more vital parts) in the crisp New England air. In our room at the Hotel Richman after the gig, Gowans opened up all the windows for fresh air. He had stripped down to his underwear. I slept wearing a sweater and overcoat!

Band leaders and booking agencies try to line up as many one-nighters as possible, because week- or month-long bookings in hotels, ballrooms and theaters don't pay nearly as well. If the jumps between gigs were 300 miles or more, we usually wouldn't even check into hotels. Many times, we got to engagements with only enough time to change clothes in the bus before the job started. The girl vocalist would try to find a ladies room to change in.

We played the hell-hole of all name bands — the Valley Arena in Holyoke, Mass. — on three separate occasions. On Saturdays and Sundays it was converted into a vaudeville house. The first time there we checked into the hotel at 4 a.m. At 8 that morning we had to begin rehearsing the multiple acts (probably about eight) that would be featured along with the band. Dorsey never attended the rehearsals or the acts' portion of the show. Herb Winfield conducted the act accompaniments. The only performers I remember from this gig were Irwin Corey, Professor Backwards (Jimmy Edmundson) and the legendary one-legged tap dancer, Pegleg Bates.

In Old Orchard Beach, Maine, we'd go out to the end of a pier where a five-gallon bucket of steamed clams with butter sauce could be purchased for 50 cents. We sat at picnic tables and drank coffee cups of whiskey to keep the chill away. We'd also get full-course lobster dinners in fine restaurants for 85 cents. Doc taught me how to pull the crustaceans apart and crack them to get to the sweetest meat.

One Saturday, a wealthy Dixieland jazz aficionado friend of Gowans took Brad and me to his Cape Cod home for a midday shore dinner. We ate and drank so much that Gowans and I dragged ourselves upstairs for a brief nap, and left explicit instructions with our host to be awakened in time to get back to the ballroom for the evening gig.

We awoke in total darkness. Our host explained that we were sleeping "like little angels," and he didn't have the heart to disturb us. We finally convinced him to quickly roll out his Lincoln and take us back, since we were already late for the job.

When we arrived, Brad explained the circumstances to Jimmy, and added, "It's all my fault, not Gene's. I take full responsibility." He handed Dorsey a beribboned cardboard box and said, "Here's a peace offering." A fuming Jimmy slammed the box down next to Helen Lee, and continued the dance set. Before we'd played two arrangements, the box lid edged up and a live lobster crawled out. It skittered back and forth across the front of the bandstand until a patron captured it. Helen almost fainted, breaking up Jimmy, and all was forgiven.

We worked a five-day stand at the King Philip Ballroom in Wrentham, Massachusetts, with wonderful room and board accommodations at the homey Stage Coach Inn. Artie and I began rooming together. After much discomfort one evening, I told him about a problem I was having. He said, "Hey, Eagle, you've just got a slight case of hemorrhoids from sitting too much and blowing too hard on the gig. It'll soon clear up." It did.

It sounds ludicrous, but the band was "family." Afternoons, we'd sometimes tramp through the autumn-leaved woods and watch the locals peddle apples and maple syrup. I kept looking for Pilgrims and Indians (to no avail).

During one intermission, Doc and Mimi "turned me on" to an enormous marijuana cigarette. Back on the bandstand, I couldn't read all those strange little spots. I was very spooked because Dorsey always pushed his music stand up against mine for six-sax stuff, and I was afraid he'd pick up on my dilemma. But when we got to my solo on *Aces Up*, I really cooked. Doc told me later that Jimmy had given me 13 choruses!

We also worked the Ritz Ballroom in Bridgeport, Connecticut; Lake Compounce in Bristol; the Armory in Danbury; the Arena in Lewiston, Maine; Canobie Lake in Salem, New Hampshire; and the Carousel Ballroom in Manchester.

Our personal luggage was dominated by several cotton broadcloth white shirts, and we could only get them laundered when we had a respite from one-nighters. Consequently, they were always filthy. Lolatte bought some of the first wash-and-wear synthetic shirts. They were perforated with tiny holes, but still held in body heat, and Bill damn near suffocated wearing them — even in the chilly New England weather.

## JD To Open At Big Club In Little City

Rochester, N. Y. — Jimmy Dorsey opens at the Club 86 in Geneva, N. Y., for one week starting November 1. Spot continues to bring all the top bands and singles to this area the year around.

Recent orks to show here have been those of Lionel Hampton, Dean Hudson, Buddy Rich, and Boyd Raeburn. Singles included Bob Eberly, Monica Lewis, Vic Damone, and others.

Geneva has population of 15,000 and is the only place in the area boasting a club that has a consistent name policy —this includes Rochester and Syracuse, with populations of some 350,000.

# JD Band Shows Wide Appeal

Rochester, N. Y.—The Dixie nucleus of the Jimmy Dorsey band, shown above, includes Charlie Teagarden, trumpet; Artie Lyons, tenor; Dorsey, clarinet, and Herd Winfield Jr., trombone. Others in the band-within-a-band, in the best Bob Cats and Clambake Seven tradition, are pianist Al Waslohn and bassist Bill Lolatte. Smaller photo shows JD vocalist Helen Lee, last pictured in the *Beat* wearing a very demure sweater. This photo, *well* . . !

# New JD Band Pleases All

Rochester, N. Y.—A fine sounding Jimmy Dorsey band, with no apparent rough spots, played a one-niter here and pleased all the fans, especially those of the old JD ork.

Even though the group played a lot of the old-style vocal numbers *a la* the Bob Eberly—Helen O'Connell combination, with Larry Nobel and Helen Lee now handling the lyrics, the band did get off a little bop now and then.

Charlie Teagarden and Ray Bauduc in the brass and rhythm sections gave a spark to ensembles, and solos of both were outstanding.

Another top man in the rhythm section is Al Waslohn, who joined the band only six weeks ago and is doing some excellent arranging in addition to piano playing.

Dorsey features a Dixieland band-within-a-band down front even though two of the group's original members, guitarist Nappy Lamare and trombonist Brad Gowans, have left. Bauduc and Teagarden pace the Dixie group including Dorsey, clarinet; Art Lyons, tenor; Herd Winfield Jr., trombone; Waslohn, piano, and Bill Lolatte, bass.
—**Jack Sheperd**

# CHAPTER 7
# DRAMATIS PERSONAE

### BRAD

Brad Gowans was the darling of the dyed-in-the-wool Dixie fans. He had played and recorded with Eddie Condon, Bud Freeman, Mezz Mezzrow, Sidney Bechet, Max Kaminsky, Dave Tough, Joe Sullivan, George Wettling, and Pee Wee Russell, to name but a few of the greats. Besides being a true eccentric, he was a mechanical genius. Not only did he invent and hand-make his combination valve and slide trombone (which was written up in *Popular Mechanics Magazine*), but he had built a car with two front ends, theoretically so he could drive the wrong way on Manhattan's one-way streets without getting a ticket! It wasn't long before every policeman in the New York area knew him, and a judge ordered him to dismantle the car.

Brad passed through Pennsylvania Station one day. An area was roped off, and a large crowd had gathered to watch President Truman arrive by train. With his valve/slide trombone hooked over his arm, Gowans elbowed his way through the throng up to a police officer. Brad told him he was Tommy Dorsey, and that he was supposed to play for the president. The dumb cop okayed it, and Brad went out on the platform.

He played Tommy Dorsey's theme song, *I'm Getting Sentimental Over You*, on his peculiar horn. Harry Truman, a pretty sharp guy, knew immediately that there was something radically wrong. Instantly, what seemed like the entire U.S. contingent of Secret Service Agents surrounded Gowans, and he was slickly escorted out of the station.

Brad, along with Doc, more or less adopted me. When we were in New York, Brad took me for food and booze at various Dixieland fans' brownstone apartments facing Washington Square in Greenwich Village.

Besides the incongruity of sporting a Boston baseball cap on the bandstand, Gowans sometimes ignored his trombone parts and read my second alto parts over my shoulder along with me. Dorsey never really objected — he was pretty easy going.

Brad collapsed while working with Eddie Skrivanek's "Sextet from Hunger" at the El Cortez Club in Las Vegas, and died of cancer in 1954 at the age of 50.

# GIBBY

Our band boy, Gibby Seaborn, had two main functions.  His basic duty was to unload the bus, and set up all the instruments, mikes, music stands and the library on the bandstand.  Sometimes, he'd even put together our saxes and clarinets.  He also unloaded our personal luggage when we checked into hotels.  Jesus, how he hated one-nighters!

Gibby's secondary role was to make sure each band member had a full Coca-Cola bottle, filled half-and-half with Coke and bourbon, under their music stand through-out the evening.  This enabled us to surreptitiously drink on the job.  Our customers must have thought we were a bunch of Coca-Cola fiends.  Gibby didn't get much of a salary, so each of us chipped in two dollars apiece every week to augment his earnings.  Later on, he had the temerity to come around with a clipboard, check off our names, and ask us to up our two-buck ante to him.  I refused, and many others must have too, because he left the band shortly after that.

# LOLATTE

Bill Lolatte, "The Italian Johnny Weissmuller," (also called "Low Life"), was a con-firmed weight lifter.  He always took a full set of weights with him on the road.  Gibby needed Bill's help to unload all that crap on "locations" (places where we stayed five days or longer), so Lolatte could work out.

In appearance, physique, demeanor, lust and lip hair, "Low Life" resembled Errol Flynn.  Before joining our group, he had been with Sarah Vaughan on Fifty Second Street.

Bill wore a hearing aid, and would overtly turn it off before all Dixie selections.  Dorsey either didn't notice, or chose to ignore it.  Also, with the spotlight on him, he would reach inside his coat and switch it off before his big featured duet with Bauduc.  Ray and Bill — all alone — were displayed every night on Bauduc's corny hit compo-sition, *Big Noise from Winnetka*.  Lolatte seldom drank, but was a connoisseur of "the weed."

# DOC

James "Doc" Clifford was 6'6" tall.  I don't think any other of our band members were over 5'11".  Doc had a somewhat withered arm that ended in a claw-like hand.  I don't know how he managed to play such fine lead alto and clarinet. When Doc, half-loaded, would lumber toward you, Frankenstein's monster would immediately come to mind, and you would feel threatened. He could be quite physical, but usually was a pussy cat. He always took care of me. He would often change parts with me so I'd have the experience of playing lead. I owe my alto "sound " to Doc. He was extremely intelligent, and may have had a real Ph.D. degree from the University of Pennsylvania.

Band leader Art Mooney contacted Doc and tried to hire our saxophone section in toto at a substantial raise in pay. Mooney had just recorded his corny big hit, *I'm Looking Over a Four-Leaf Clover*, and wanted to improve his orchestra. Doc told him, "We aren't interested in joining your Mickey Mouse extravaganza!"

Doc was killed in the '50s when his Volkswagen "Bug" collided with a semi truck outside of Las Vegas.

### MIMI

Mimi La Rocca, "The Italian Hillbilly," was a manic Sicilian — the "Rudolph Valentino" of the band. He had large, glistening, moist eyes and black, curly hair. High-class women in the audience would send notes up to him ..... "I want to go to bed with you." Any kind of "high" was great with Mimi, and he had no qualms about mixing two or three at a time. He wore a fuzzy porkpie hat and, unfortunately, chewed garlic cloves while we were on the bus.

We once stopped at a cafeteria in Steubenville, Ohio. Upon entering, Mimi spotted a young lady seated alone, and zeroed in on her. Her table was covered with a large cloth. La Rocca immediately crawled underneath. The girl was so stunned and embarrassed by Mimi's intrusion, it was some time before she managed to stand up. If any of the rest of us had tried anything like that, we'd have ended up in jail, or would have been shot on the spot!

One night, in the Cafe Rouge of the Pennsylvania Hotel in Manhattan, we had a trans-continental radio hook-up. We opened with *Green Eyes*. Shortly after the intro, the baritone sax had some notes all alone. Mimi screwed it up. Dorsey stopped the band and announced to the world over the mike, "Our baritone saxophonist, Mimi La Rocca, loused it up, so we are going to begin again." For months after that, Mimi got fan mail from such places as Brazil, Argentina and Peru.

If Mimi is still alive at this writing, it's a miracle!

## BAUDUC

Other than being a renowned Dixieland drummer from New Orleans, Ray's forte was his ability to sleep anywhere at any time. While the rest of us would be hassling to check in at a hotel, he'd calmly sit down in the lobby and immediately fall asleep. We were all envious of this talent during our long, wide-eyed hours on the bus.

Once, after sleeping for several hours on the bus, Bauduc awoke, looked out at the miles of cornfields, and said to our driver, Charlie Mucci, "You're going the wrong way." We pooh-poohed him, and told him to go the hell back to sleep. Later, Mucci discovered that we had gone 90 miles in the wrong direction. Old Bauduc had been on the road for so many years, he probably knew every cow pasture in the Midwest.

Ray had a tendency to rush tempos, and being basically a fine New Orleans-type drummer, was out of his element when we played bop-styled arrangements. Dorsey was always ragging Ray with remarks such as, "With you, a beat is a vegetable!"

Bauduc was quite an inventor. He had patents on many drum accessories manufactured by the Slingerland Company. For the Avedis Zildjian Company, Ray invented the "sizzle" cymbal, which had loose rivets inserted around the edges. He also designed the "Speed King" foot pedal for the Ludwig Company. He would periodically receive royalty checks from these firms.

I'm sure Ray kept the first nickel he ever earned.

## MASSO

Our lead trombonist, George Masso, left the band after a year to return to college. Jimmy compared, usually unfavorably, every lead trombonist to brother Tommy and to Bobby Byrne. However, George was one of the few ever entrusted with the extremely high solo on Sonny Burke's fine arrangement of *Lover*. Before Masso, the last person to be given the solo had been Moe Zudicoff (Buddy Morrow) in 1945. The solo was usually delegated to a trumpet player — even on the recording.

## LORRAINE

Al Lorraine succeeded Masso. On his starting night, the first tune Dorsey called out was *Lover*. We all thought Al did a wonderful job on it, but evidently Jimmy didn't. From then on, Charlie Teagarden played it on trumpet.

Lorraine never drank, but was stoned on "grass" from wakening until retiring. He taught us how to make a paper funnel (the large opening went over the face), and smoke marijuana through a trombone slide. We were quite taken with this for a while. He talked v-e-r-y s-l-o-w-l-y in an ultra-hip manner. Such statements as, "Like, I mean, wow, you know, man?," soon started to make sense. Come to think of it, his meaning was actually crystal-clear if we were on the same level of "highness."

### ARTIE

Artie Lyons was usually "on the wagon," and as copyist for arrangers Waslohn and Gibeling, was kept pretty busy. However, he did manage to go on a tear at times. Lyons played wonderfully liquid "Artie Shaw style" jazz clarinet, but was relegated to playing tenor in the Dixie ensemble.

Someone nicknamed him "Humphrey," after the short, chunky, put-upon character in the Gasoline Alley comic strip. Whenever he would start moaning and groaning on the bus, we'd whine back in unison, "Poor Humphrey!"

Artie frequented the finest restaurants, but usually ordered a raw steak. The waitresses and chefs always got frustrated, and would beg to "just heat it up a little," but he was adamant.

Since Lyons never got a chance to shine on clarinet, we sought out an after-hours joint where we could jam. We found one, and were busy cranking out some damn passable jazz, when the owner came out from behind the bar. He put a clarinet together and proceeded to blow us all away. To this day, the only thing I know about him is his name — Billy Cretchmer. Poor Humphrey — upstaged again!

Artie and I were staying at the Hotel Belvedere in New York. Phil Cenicola invited us to his mother's Brooklyn home for an authentic Italian dinner. Artie decided to celebrate by having *one* glass of wine in the hotel bar. After several (15?) in several bars, we ended up in a "French-Communist" hangout under the 3rd Avenue "El". Lyons understood some French, and told me the regulars were calling us capitalist pigs, and that we should get the hell out of there.

Back at the Belvedere, we stumbled around before I decided to sober up in the shower prior to our dinner engagement. I passed out over the drain; water had begun to rise in the stall before a reeling Artie clawed me out. Mama Cenicola and son Phil ate without us that night.

On one of our infrequent nights off, some of us decided to "fete" Lyons. We went to hear the great blind pianist Art Tatum at a club in Pittsburgh. It had a revolving stage featuring continuous entertainment; a small bop combo was playing as we entered. The alto man brought their set to a close with a four-measure flourish of sixteenth notes. As the stage turned around, Tatum played that passage exactly — with the left hand — while playing a slow ballad with his right. Within a few seconds, he had let everyone know who was boss!

I went to see Tatum every chance I could. I would shake his hand and say, "Hello, Art." On hearing my voice he would reply, "Hello, Gene." He must have known hundreds of people by their voices.

(Eerily, as I was typing this segment, I received a 'phone call from my buddy, trumpet man Jack Trott, informing me that Arthur J. Lyons had just passed away.)

### *CHOLLY*

Charlie "Little T" Teagarden (brother Jack was "Big T") was a sweet man and an exceptional trumpeter. He had played with innumerable name bands, including Paul Whiteman. His big vocal numbers (he sang like Jack) were *Big Butter and Egg Man, Charlie, My Boy* and *I Can't Get Started with You*. On the latter, he often paraphrased the lyrics to fit the occasion. If Tommy Dorsey was present, Charlie would parody the lyrics by singing, "I've been consulted by Jimmy D., and I've been insulted by Tommy D."

Teagarden was quite obese, and managed to put away two quarts of Imperial Whiskey a day. No wonder he married a nurse.

In Montevideo, Minnesota, some of us decided to have breakfast in the hotel dining room before going to bed. Hell, it was 8 a.m. We spontaneously broke into laughter when we spotted a familiar character actor, Jack Norton, at the next table. He had done the same "drunk bit" in some 20 films. He would shove about 15 cigarettes into his mouth, and all of them would eventually fall out, except one. He would then nonchalantly light the remaining cigarette. We congregated around his table, and Dick Hoffman put a pack of butts down while we cajoled Norton into doing his specialty.

Our laughter intensified and became completely uncontrolled when we spied Cholly through the window, braced against a terrible snowstorm, heading back from the liquor store.

31

At the sight of "Little T," even Norton broke up. I'll never know why the management didn't evict us — I guess there's safety in numbers and quasi-fame.

## PHIL

In Canada, I roomed with Phil Cenicola. He was very naive and staid, didn't drink or smoke, and had none of our other "minor" vices. He was even true to his wife. Most Canadian hotels had one bathroom between every two rooms. Mimi and Doc had the adjoining room. Although Mimi could appropriate almost any high-class woman, he was sometimes partial to low-level hookers. Late one night, he sneaked one of them into our room and had her kneel over the face of a sleeping Phil. Then we woke Cenicola up (rim shot!). Phil didn't speak to any band member for four days after that!

Dorsey was always needling Phil. Although Cenicola was a marvelous flute player, Jimmy almost had him convinced that he couldn't play it at all. Dorsey would sometimes have Phil purchase reeds for him, and then tell him there wasn't a good one in the whole box.

On Jimmy's very difficult specialty, *Fingerbustin'*, he would sometimes have Phil play the last high note on flute if Dorsey felt that he couldn't hit it that night. One magical evening, Dick pulverized two bennies in Phil's cup of coffee. Cenicola soon became unusually animated. When Dorsey motioned to him to take the high note, Phil stood up and took a long chorus.

We took Benzedrine only when it was essential that we stay awake; marijuana was strictly a recreational drug. Booze was a necessity. It got you through the job, and allowed you to sleep on the bus or in strange hotel rooms.

## ROMANO

Al "The Mouse" Romano, Jimmy's driver and bodyguard, was a weird one — and a bed-wetter. When he was introduced to someone and if they said, "How do you do?," he would gruffly reply, "How do I do what?" He thought that was hilarious. He always seemed to be "on stage" in an attempt to be a toady or court jester for Dorsey. I roomed with him twice. There was something about him that spooked me.

Once, while I was seated at a lunch counter, he came up behind me, pulled my coat down over my arms (a gangster's way to incapacitate a person), yanked me to the floor, and began to beat me up. Artie and Mimi saved me. Al couldn't come up with a logical reason for his outburst. He just said, "Gene's getting too uppity." Maybe my wearing of mirrored sunglasses and a Sinatra "floppy" bow tie on the bus that day set him off.

The enigma of Romano was finally solved in 1953, when Artie Lyons sent me an article from *The Los Angeles Times*. It stated that, after an extended drinking binge, Al had given himself up to the Hollywood police station and confessed to a 1942 murder. He maintained that he had shot a man with a .38 caliber pistol in a New York City hotel room, stuffed the body in a drum case, and transported it to a vacant lot in Brooklyn, where he burned it. A New York police detective was contacted by the L.A. police, and he was able to verify the facts.

No wonder Romano spooked me. The moral: Be very selective in choosing a room-mate!

### JIMMY

The sax section was constantly astounded by Dorsey's amazing technique, especially on his antiquated Albert System (fingering mechanism) clarinet. He once had a half-Albert, half-Boehm System clarinet specially made for him by the Selmer Company in Paris when he was touring Europe with the Ted Lewis band in the 1920s. He thought the instrument would facilitate an eventual switch over to the more modern Boehm System, but he couldn't make the change. Jimmy finally gave the clarinet to Eddie Miller.

I once took his clarinet in for repairs and said to the repair man, "Be careful, this belongs to Jimmy Dorsey." The guy answered, "How could I hurt it? How the hell does he manage to play this piece of shit anyway?"

Thomas F. Dorsey, Sr. had taught his sons well. He worked in the coal mines and instructed the boys on various musical instruments so that they could escape the mines. Jimmy, the oldest, was born on February 29, 1904 in Shenandoah, Pennsylvania, and grew up in nearby Langsford. (Tommy was born on November 19, 1905.) The brothers learned music early on, and played in their father's band for parades and concerts.

Pop Dorsey started both of his sons on slide trumpet, later switching Jimmy to C Melody sax and cornet, and Tommy to mellophone, tenor sax and trombone. At age

12, Jimmy played the difficult cornet solo on *Carnival of Venice* at the Langsford town pavilion. Jimmy doubled on trumpet until the late '30s. I still have some early recordings in which Jimmy sounds like famed cornetist Bix Beiderbecke.

Jimmy briefly worked in the mines along with fellow musician Russ Morgan before organizing the Wild Canary Orchestra. In the early '20s, he moved on to the Scranton Sirens, and talked the leader into hiring Tommy. This routine continued as Jimmy progressed through the bands of the California Ramblers, Jean Goldkette and Paul Whiteman. Beginning about 1925, the brothers freelanced in New York and became established as excellent section players and hot soloists. Jimmy toured Europe with Ted Lewis in mid-1920, and became immediately successful as a band leader in 1935.

After years of getting together musicians for "casuals," the battling Dorseys organized their first permanent orchestra in 1934. It was a great band, and far ahead of it's time. Early members were Freddy Slack, Glenn Miller, Bob Crosby, Bunny Berigan, Bob Eberly, Ray McKinley and Charlie Spivak.

In the following year, the Dorseys landed at the top big band spot in the country — the Glen Island Casino in New Rochelle, New York.

While playing there on Memorial Day, Tommy's Irish temper and Jimmy's needling came to a head. Tommy counted off the tempo for *I'll Never Say Never Again, Again*. Jimmy said, "Isn't that a little fast, Mac?" Tommy glared at him, picked up his trombone, and stalked off the bandstand — never to return.

Both brothers transposed by clef, and could improvise in any key. Many of Jimmy's solos were in four and five sharps. Tommy and Jimmy couldn't get along at all, but always stood up for each other. As grown men, they would often get into fist fights. When they were together, Jimmy called Tommy "Mac," and Tommy called Jimmy "Lad." Separately, each referred to the other as "The Brother." They finally made up when Tommy Sr., on his deathbed, asked them to.

Jimmy was intrigued by bebop, but never with an idea of altering his style — thank God! He was only interested in the chord structure and sequence. He once paid Charlie Parker $100 to play all night for him in his hotel room. When I bopped, he used to say to me, "I don't know what the hell you're doing, but I like it."

Many musicians questioned Dorsey's wavy vibrato and limpid sound on solos, but he used a straight, strong sound when playing lead on six-sax arrangements. However, no one questioned his astonishing technique and knowledge of chord changes, and interestingly, both Parker and Lester Young mentioned him as one of their favorite saxophonists. Oddly, Jimmy played sax and clarinet from the right side of his mouth, and trumpet from the left. Charlie Frasier, Jimmy's long-time road manager and flutist, maintained that Dorsey injured his lip from long hours of trumpet practice, which was the reason for the embouchure switch.

Dorsey had been a member of the great Paul Whiteman orchestra of the late '20s that included Tommy, Bix Beiderbecke, Matty Malneck, Bing Crosby, Henry Busse, Ferde Grofé, Frankie Trumbauer, Bill Challis and Joe Venuti. Jimmy played the opening clarinet cadenza on Gershwin's new composition, *Rhapsody in Blue*, and was featured on his own composition, *Oodles of Noodles*. Our theme song, *Contrasts*, was taken from the slow movement of that piece. Freddy Slack wrote the arrangement.

One night, a pixilated Bing Crosby showed up with a Navy WAVE in tow. He was sans toupee, and nobody recognized him. He asked Jimmy if he could sing with the band. Dorsey said, "Hell, no! You're too bombed, and it would ruin your goddamned image!"

Two overly extroverted movie stars — Mickey Rooney and Dan Dailey — would often sit in with the band, though. And both were crappy drummers! We hated to see them enter the room when we were playing. Bauduc would get especially upset at their intrusion.

We almost never rehearsed, but when we did, Jimmy would spend half the time telling stories about Bix, Joe Venuti and Joe Frisco, the stuttering comedian. We thought the jokes he told were odious, and he would break up when the brass section would throw mutes at him.

Dorsey loved telling one about his valet, Al "The Champ" Joslow, who was an ex-boxer who had taken a few too many punches to the head. It had to do with Joslow being in a heated argument with someone, when, in exasperation, the guy finally said, "What are you, a connoisseur?" To which Al replied, "No, I ain't sore."

But on the job, unless he was drinking heavily, Dorsey could be a complete perfectionist. If you screwed up, he might be all over your ass. Once, and only once, Little T and Maynard Ferguson traded choruses, each trying to play in the other's style.

Jimmy was furious. He said that they were hired to play in their own original styles — PERIOD!

During a dinner set at the Deshler-Wallick Hotel in Columbus, Ohio (we were playing a rather sedate Gershwin medley), a dowager sent up a note asking us to mute the brass. Dorsey sent one back to her: "Why don't you eat at the Neal House? They have a goddamned string quartet." He then signaled Maynard to play his solo, *It Ain't Necessarily So* up an octave.

At Virginia Tech in Blacksburg, a drunk kept heckling Jimmy. The lush finally uttered the magic words: he asked if Jimmy was Tommy Dorsey's brother. With that, Jimmy hit him over the head with his clarinet. Dorsey was later arrested, posted a $100 bond for an appearance in Richmond, and was released.

Many bandleaders (Artie Shaw, Tommy Dorsey and Benny Goodman come to mind) would consistently ignore the 12 or so rows of high school and college fans crowded around the bandstand. Les Brown was, and still is, an exception. He would talk to everyone and have the entire band sign autographs.

Jimmy was the same. If the crowd was especially receptive, during intermissions Romano would bring out a chair, a glass of Dewars and water, some Old Gold cigarettes, Jimmy's gold Dunhill lighter and his glasses. With that, Dorsey would sit down and autograph various pieces of paper and 8x10s for the entire break. That's class!

Funny, the whole band referred to Jimmy as "The Old Man." He was all of 45! Who could believe he would be dead in eight years?

PRESTO

**REALLY, doubling in BRASS**

Brad Gowans uses slide and valve simultaneously on his new "valide" trombone.

Close-up of valve assembly (below) shows thumb holding key that locks first valve.

This Young Man's Horn Does Two Horns' Work

*for ½ man's pay*

Bᴿᴬᴰ Gowans cites the musical passage above as one that can be played only on one trombone—the Valide, combination valve and slide instrument that he invented and built. Known to millions as an outstanding "hot" musician, Gowans is not widely renowned for the fine machinist he also is.

Since 1922, Gowans has played the slide trombone, clarinet, cornet, saxophone, drums, piano, ballad horn and valve trombone with 27 groups, including The Original Dixieland Jazz Band. He is now playing the Valide in Eddie Condon's band. On the Valide 28 notes can be played in one position without changing the embouchure (position of the mouth against the mouthpiece) as against seven on any other trombone; it can be used as a slide trombone in seven keys by locking down the valves in different combinations, as a valve trombone in four keys by locking the slide in one of its four positions, as a valide by using both methods

at once or one in conjunction with the other. The thumb of the left hand operates the valve lock to add the fifth, sixth and seventh positions to the four-position slide. The middle finger of the left hand holds the slide and tunes the valves when the right hand is being used on the valves. The right hand operates both valves and slide. Where fast changes are involved the thumb and little finger control the slide while the second, third and fourth fingers work the valves.

Other advantages: Valve assembly is moved up close to mouthpiece, relieving player's arms of much weight; short slide avoids danger of smashing slide into some obstacle; many arpeggios impossible of execution on slide trombone can be played; chromatic passages can be played faster; glissando is easier of execution; embouchure is not disturbed when slide is fully extended.

Gowans will not market the instrument, at least not until he finishes a new contract recording for Victor with his own band.

This Young Man (Really) With A Horn also recently perfected a realistic parlor baseball game after 25 years' work. Right now he is installing a 91-cubic-inch, 8-cylinder racing engine in a British Standard Swallow. After he finishes playing with Condon at 4 a.m., that is.

*Bray*

*Dick—There is a way to do anything if you believe it!*

37

**Doc - "Professional Lover"**

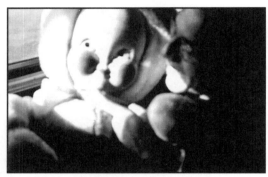

**George Masso and Girlfriend**

## Sidemen Switches

Three new trombone men with Sammy Kaye: Frank Webb, Gil Stancourt, and Jimmy Dell. Don Plumby and Frank Hutchinson exited . . . Trumpet men Louis Mucci and Billy Howell joined Miguelito Valdes . . . Al Lorraine, trombone, has taken George Masso's chair with Jimmy Dorsey.

**"Like, I mean, you know?"**
**Mimi and Doc learning to talk jive**
**like Al Lorraine**

38

**Chuck and Mimi**

Gibby Seaborn has one of the most important jobs in the organization. He is the propertty manager and keeps tab on all the equipment, loads and unloads the bus the troupe uses and sets up the stage. He dreads one-night stands.

# CHAPTER 8
# ROAD RASCALS

### WASHINGTON, D.C.

We drew 6,000 people for a one-nighter at the Uline Arena in Washington, D.C. We had the following day off, and the Teagardens invited me to have oysters with them on the shores of the Potomac. I declined, and opted for a movie that night.

At that time, Washington was completely racially segregated, with separate hotels, restaurants, rest rooms, drinking fountains and waiting rooms. At home, in San Diego, if you wanted to smoke in a theater, you sat in the balcony, so I bought an upstairs ticket. Immediately, the ticket seller and several people in line behind me informed me that I had purchased a "nigger" ticket. I pleaded ignorance (ha!), and exchanged it for an acceptable "white" one.

### MASSACHUSETTS

In Boston, I would continually get lost going from the Avery Hotel to the theater, which was only three blocks away. The city had originally been designed in a circular fashion by some misguided architect, and had never recovered. Paul Clifton, a friend of mine, told me that when he was in the Navy he took many expensive cab trips from that hotel to Ruby Foo's Restaurant. One night, he said to his date, "Let's go to Ruby Foo's — I'll get a taxi." She replied, "What for? It's only a couple of blocks away."

Every time we were in Boston, Mimi and I wanted to go out to Fenway Park to see manager Joe McCarthy's Red Sox, which starred Birdie Tibbets, Johnny Pesky, Ted Williams, Bobby Doerr, Dominic DiMaggio and Pat Dobson, but we were always hung with theater dates.

### PENNSYLVANIA

You could smell chocolate a mile before arriving in a tasty Hershey, Pa. All the businesses and housing were owned by the Hershey Chocolate Company, and most of the adults in the town were employed by the factory. Hershey Park Ballroom had free admission. Talk about a company town and a closed shop!

In Uniontown, some "green hipsters" kept harassing Dorsey about the "corny" music we were supposedly playing. They kept bugging us to play some modern bebop. Jimmy finally said, "O-k-a-y boys — here's some bop." He called up a middle-'30s arrangement of *John Silver*, and the "hep cats" ate it up. So much for music appreciation classes in the school systems of our nation!

## CONNECTICUT

We played a one-nighter in a downstairs ballroom at Yale University in New Haven. Hal McIntyre's band was playing upstairs. While we were warming up, Dorsey came over to me and said, "Don't worry about your goddamned transportation home — I'LL PAY FOR IT!" We got into a hell of an argument. He thought I had been mocking him during some of my solos and warm-ups. That wasn't true. I loved him — and his playing. I ended up crying. Not too cool for a 23-year-old! We finally patched things up, and he brought McIntyre down to hear me play.

## NEW JERSEY

Somewhere in New Jersey, a guy came up to me and said, "Hey, you're Bud Shank. I heard youse on the radd-io. Where do youse go from here, hey?" I tried to convince him that I wasn't Bud, but he kept insisting, "Yes, you are! Yes, you are!" I finally gave up, signed Bud Shank's autograph, and escaped.

## NEW YORK

Via the old GAC dartboard, we were booked into Saranac Lake, in the upper reaches of New York state — near the Canadian border — after performing in New York City the previous night. Obviously, the bus was incapable of achieving this objective, so Dorsey chartered a DC-3 airliner. Once airborne, we fell and soared and soared and fell as we encountered incredible turbulence (called "air pockets" back then) all across the Adirondack Mountains. Although most of us were confirmed agnostics, we all got "that old-time religion" during the flight. The worst part was knowing we had to do it all over again after the gig — at night!

Way out on Long Island one night, we played "Regula's Corner" — a black night-club. I don't know why GAC booked us there (probably got us confused with Lucky Millinder), but the patrons really dug us. Dorsey pulled out all of our best jazz charts. We sat at their tables during intermission and drank what the blacks called "nigger cocktails" — gin and Coca-Cola.

41

## ILLINOIS

Contemplating a long bus ride from New York to Chicago, Artie and I, drunk with wealth, opted for the train. We checked into the Croydon Hotel in the Windy City's "loop" long before the others were due and went across the street to "scarf" some barbecued ribs. I kept ogling a woman seated alone at a nearby table. As we left, I put my hotel key on her table. She came to my room that evening. During the night, my roomy, Dick, arrived. He insisted that we let him into the room so he could go to bed. He kept whining, "Please — I promise not to watch!"

(About a week later, I developed a penile discharge. I was sure I had contracted some sort of "galloping crud" from that lady. When we finally passed through a town large enough to maintain a physician, I hot-footed it to his office. He assured me I just had a "strain.")

One night, Jimmy went up and down the hotel corridors waking us, and herding us to his room. A nude and nubile blonde was seated, cross-legged, on the rug with Dorsey's hernia belt on her head. She kept repeating, "I don't hear anything." Jimmy whispered to us that he had told her it was a shortwave radio.

We worked Rockford on a New Year's Eve. We all got smashed, and traded horns for the coast-to-coast broadcast. What a fiasco! I recall that four saxophonists tried to play trumpet, Jimmy played flute and Charlie played Dorsey's alto. The dancers didn't seem to mind, but I'm sure the radio audience was aghast.

Doc suggested that he and I should put away tunes we had memorized. Eventually, we didn't bother to unpack all 400 arrangements. Of course, once in every blue moon, Jimmy would throw us a curve and call up some obscure 1930-40 chart, and we'd scuffle like mad. Question: Why do band leaders insist on calling out tunes by their titles, when each score has a perfectly legible number written in the upper right-hand corner (i.e., *Oh, What a Beautiful Morning* was number 1143). Answer: Hell, they've already found it — now it's your turn!

## WISCONSIN

We were at a theater in Madison, home of the University of Wisconsin, for a week. The chairman of the science department, an old "head," was a real weirdo. He would have fit in perfectly on the faculty at the University of California at Berkeley during the '60s. He was always underfoot during our week's gig. He was experimenting with different strains of marijuana, trying to develop the *perfect* plant, so he continually tried new varieties on us. Also, he kept hounding us to go down to the power station and jam with the machinery. That was even too far out for us, but we continued to smoke his "muggles" — which were terrible.

### *MICHIGAN*

When we got to Detroit, my dad's brother, Forrest, took Phil and me to dinner at an "Oh, so-English" restaurant in the Book-Cadillac Hotel.

We had a "battle of the bands" that night with the Tex Beneke Orchestra at the Detroit Arena. We alternated sets and pretty much ignored one another, not attempting to activate any big guns. Finally, Tex decided it was time to scare us. He featured Pete Condoli, doing the "Superman" trumpet routine (complete with cape) which Pete had originated with the Woody Herman band. Dorsey countered with an unknown Maynard Ferguson, playing notes from outer space! That brought the entire Beneke aggregation up to our bandstand.

Since Maynard was underage, his parents and older brother, Mike, followed the bus in their old Ford with its previous year's license plates (I think they were all living off Ferguson's salary). They watched him like hawks, but didn't know that Helen Lee and Clare Hogan, in turn, had already seduced him. Maynard was kind of a jerk, had the personality of a steamed clam, and really didn't play much jazz; but you could never criticize his ability to hit notes only pit bulls could hear.

Many years later, I was talking to Wally Millford, a friend in San Diego, and we discovered that he had been playing baritone sax that night with the Beneke group. Small world!

The Indiana Roof, Indianapolis, Indiana

# CHAPTER 9
## CANADIAN CAPERS

From Detroit, we crossed the border to Windsor, Ontario. We were held up by Canadian customs agents for three hours while they searched every piece of luggage. We thought they were looking for drugs, but the initial culprit turned out to be Brad's weird trombone. Seems it had no brand name or serial number on it. Holy Christ — and these guys were supposed to be our "friendly" neighbors!

We played look-alike ballrooms in Peterborough, Toronto, Niagara Falls and Crystal Beach. They each resembled Hollywood movie sets, complete with multi-tiered bandstands replete with fountains and waterfalls. In a huge auditorium in Quebec City we played a concert where not a soul understood English, but they loudly cheered the vocal renditions of *Green Eyes, Maria Elena, Amapola* and *Tangerine*.

We had three nights at Danceland Ballroom in Montreal, and stayed at the ultra-swank Laurentian Hotel. Hoffman insisted that, since Montreal was situated in southern Canada, it should be called "Montre-you-all."

I met a girl at the gig, got a cab, and went to her apartment on the outskirts of town. I was unable to find a taxi when I left her place and had to trudge back to the hotel in a snow storm. I reached the Laurentian at 4 a.m. When I got off the elevator, there were several people and the bell captain (who was dressed like a Nazi general) clustered around my room. I was told that the entire floor was being kept awake, and if I didn't do something about my roommate, we would be evicted. I entered the room and, honest to God, Brad was doing four things at once: taking a bath, eating a room-service dinner, practicing his trombone and talking long distance to actor Dick Foran in Hollywood! I convinced him to do just three things, and order was restored.

Soon after that, it became evident to both Dorsey and Gowans that a change had to be made, and Brad went back to New York to get fitted for dentures and try to locate his mind. Artie received a telegram from Brad a few days later. It was encoded thusly:

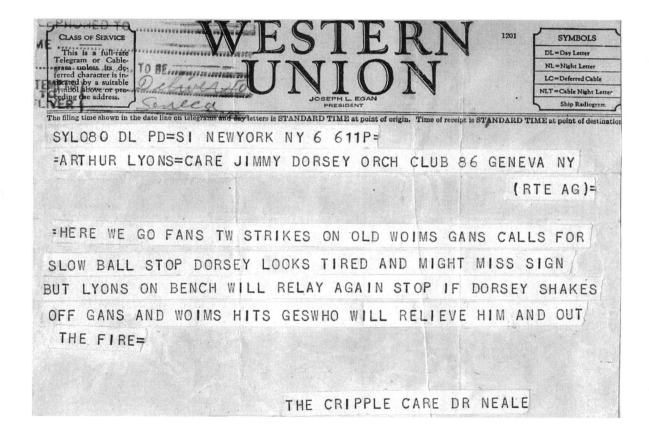

**Telegram
from Brad Gowens**

# Canadian Customs

**A band boy, Mimi and Artie;
Alvin is debarking**

**Cenicola, Dorsey, Romano**

**Phil
Al Lorraine
Herb
Teagarden
Noble**

**Noble, Cenicola, Lolatte**

**Canadian customs inspector**

**Dorsey          Gil**

# CHAPTER 10
# HOTEL HELLIONS

Back in those days, hotels issued keys with a large name tag attached. You were supposed to turn in your key whenever you left the hotel. This facilitated maid service and let the management know that you weren't "at home." We never did that. Consequently, I have 60 hotel keys complete with name tags mounted on a nice piece of plywood in my garage. Some of those hotel room numbers evoke quite nostalgic feelings!

Hoffman and Graves had some sort of misunderstanding, so I started rooming with Dick. That was a mistake! He was a *dedicated* boozer. Every intermission, he would consume three Manhattans and a beer chaser. After work, he'd start in on serious drinking. He'd come into the hotel room very late, make a lot of noise taking his clothes off, flop into bed and almost immediately begin to snore vociferously.

One night, I had a few drinks and sulked alone in the room for a while. Finally, I disassembled every stick of furniture except my bed, and put it all out in the hall. I then bolted the door from the inside, and hit the sack.

Gil cornered me in the lobby the next morning and said, "Gene, you are always such a gentlemen. What happened to you last night? My daughter will soon be on vacation from the Catholic girls' school she attends, and I was going to introduce you to her. I think I've just changed my mind." Oh well, what the hell — she probably looked like Lila anyway!

Some hotel managers told us never to check into their establishments again. Doc's pet peeve was radios that only operated if you inserted a quarter. He invariably threw them against the wall when he checked out. Also, he once managed to shove a dresser out of the 14th floor window just to hear the wonderful sound it made when it smashed into the courtyard below. The only one able to upstage Doc was Dodo Marmaroso, who, while with the Charlie Barnet band, proceeded to push a piano off a mezzanine into a hotel lobby!

One delerious night, four of us got into an insane water fight using the long fire hoses that adorned hotel hallways in those days. Little T and Florence intervened, and sent us to bed . Bad, bad boys!

# CHAPTER 11
# FOOD FOR THOUGHT

Five of the band members and our driver were first-generation Italian-Americans. They took pots, pans and other culinary paraphernalia with them on the road. The kitchen supplies would be unloaded whenever we stayed in one place for longer than five days. Lolatte, Masso, Cenicola, Romano, La Rocca and the bus driver, Charlie Mucci, would then scour the community for a stove, and immediately start a spaghetti sauce in an enormous pot. The melange had to simmer for 12 hours, and every once in a while one of the Guineas would look into the cauldron — maybe drop something else in — and replace the lid. They were very clannish, and never divulged their recipe, but the result was the best damned spaghetti I've ever eaten.

Al Romano was a skilled chef. On location jobs, he would often use the kitchen in the hotel or club to whip up things like Chicken Cacciatore for us to scarf while we worked the gig.

We'd go from the culinary ridiculous to the sublime. We ate in either greasy diners or the finest restaurants. Whenever our horde of 23 people descended on some tiny all-night truck stop diner, Romano would go back into the kitchen to speed things up. The help would always object, but Al would merely tell them that we were famous, and on a strict time schedule, and would then go on about his business. He would sometimes even wait on the local-yokel counter trade. I remember one customer ordering a steak sandwich. Al sawed off the end of a broom and served it to him on a bun!

Bitchy Bauduc was always a time-consuming hang-up. His eggs had to be exactly one-and-one-half minutes on each side, basted in butter, with home fries, dry medium bacon, and medium whole wheat toast on the side. If it wasn't served that way, he'd send it back, and we'd all lay into him for his idiosyncratic attitude. On leaving the eatery, we usually told the gape-mouthed patrons we were either a basketball team or the Hal McIntyre orchestra.

On departing one of these greasy spoons, Joe Graves liberated a large peanut machine into which he hoped to dip for a late-night snack. About three miles out of town a state trooper pulled the bus over. Dorsey explained that no member of his fine, upstanding organization could be guilty of such a dastardly deed, but the officer went directly to the back of the bus, gently moved Edna aside, and confiscated the machine. The gendarme collected a $50 bribe from Jimmy and sent us on our way. I'm sure the entire hick-town population heaved a collective sigh of relief to be rid of these strange, alien beings.

Once, Charlie Barnet's band decided to forego their bus, and travel from Cleveland to Buffalo by boat. They drunkenly congregated at the stern of the vessel and began throwing glasses, ice buckets and bottles overboard. This became so much fun, that they graduated to tossing deck chairs into the deep. An over-wrought purser came charging up to Barnet. "Whose band is this?" he indignantly shouted. "Jimmy Dorsey's," replied Charlie.

# CHAPTER 12
# THE VOGUE TERRACE

After a string of murderous one-nighters, we were booked for six nights at the Vogue Terrace Ballroom of the Alpine Hotel in McKeesport, Pennsylvania — across the river from Pittsburgh. Conveniently, our rooms were in the same hotel.

After hours, many of us would sit in the dark ballroom and listen to Al Waslohn play his latest classical "Chopinesque" piano compositions. Tutti "Toots" Camarata, who had arranged for Dorsey, was then leading a symphonic-type recording orchestra in England. Jimmy sent some of Waslohn's opuses to Toots, who arranged them; they were then recorded by an English orchestra. I believe Al was in some way connected with the Cincinnati Symphony years later. I do know that he was musical director for "The Coffee Club" on television, had a symphony performed by the Columbus Symphony, and his pop tune, *While Stephanie Sleeps*, was recorded by Johnny Mathis. Waslohn died at the early age of 51.

A major Pittsburgh newspaper sent a reporter and photographer over to the hotel to interview band members. They spent all day and evening with us. We fought like little kids to get in the pictures and to be interviewed. They published a three-page feature spread on the band. Looking back, I'm glad I bought a copy of the paper at the time.

During intermission one night, I met a young lady in the bar. She invited me to her parents' home in Pittsburgh for Thanksgiving dinner. If you can, picture an "effete," suit-and-tie bedecked dance band musician sitting at the dinner table with mom and pop and four huge "steel-worker" big brothers wearing undershirts. Needless to say, I was afraid to even hold hands with that girl.

About this time, Jimmy had Neal Hefti and Howard Gibeling write some bebop originals featuring a "band within a band" for Maynard, trombonist Chuck Maxon (who had replaced Brad Gowans) and me. *Aces Up, Seesaw* and *Diz Does Everything* were added to the library, and I finally had solo opportunities on five tunes. We also received some charts from Dizzy Gillespie (one was *Grand Central Getaway*), but they were extremely difficult, so Jimmy got Diz to drop by and rehearse us.

Herb Winfield from New York City and George Masso of North Providence R.I., two members of the trombone section, cut out some clippings to send home.

The maestro in the business tunes up

## Jimmy Dorsey's Outfit Typical of Successful Dance Orchestras

Jimmy Dorsey's band, now playing at the Vogue Terrace of the Alpine Hotel, is typical of the successful bigtime dance orchestras. All the business and personnel work required in any other enterprise are tied in with the job of arraning and playing.

Everyone has plenty to do, whether it's during the show, rehearsing or making preparations to move from one job to another. The photos here show some of the members of the Dorsey organization.

Helen Lee, vocalist from Mobile, ALa., displays some of the expensive gowns she wears while singing with the band.

Dick Hoffman, left, trumpet player from Springfield, N.Y., and Larry Noble, vocalist, look over a score.

Right, Ray Bauduc, one of the top drummer men, is shown with a section of the band as they play a number.

Gilbert Koerner, business manager. A musician, he is the busiest man in the outfit, handling all the expense accounts, salaries and other financial problems.

Herb

J.D.

Artie

Ray

Gene

Charlie

Dorsey reherses a specialty number with Charlie Teagarden, outstanding trumpet player, right and other members of the band.

# There's More Than Music in Running a Band

Take it from Jimmy Dorsey, the man who knows, a big name band isn't all sweet music.

Behind those jazzy tunes is a compact business organization wound up in all the red tape connected with any enterprise.

Now playing at the Vogue Terrace of the Alpine Hotel, Jimmy Dorsey and his band exemplify what it takes to make a band a "big name" outfit, as well as a stable, paying business proposition.

**Business Manager**

The Jimmy Dorsey organization consists of an agent for the road, a business manager, personnel manager, musicians, arrangers, vocalists, and Bandleader Dorsey.

Each of the men associated with the band has plenty of work to keep him busy, whether the outfit is on the stage or preparing for the next show.

Take, for example, Personnel Manager Gilbert Koerner, whom Dorsey describes as "the busiest man in the gang."

Koerner is an ex-musician as well as a businessman. He arranges all radio programs, worries along with members of the band over their problems, takes care of all expense accounts and entertainment.

"Koerner," says Dorsey, "is our figure expert. Anything that pertains to money or figures we give to him."

One night stands are dreaded by the property man, Gibby Seaborn. It's his job to keep watch on all equipment, to load and reload the bus in which the troupe travels, and to set up the stage, including wiring, microphones, music stands, etc.

Personnel Manager Koerner also handles all the finances for the band. He pointed out:

"A lot of people are impressed by the fancy sums a band like ours demands for a performance. But behind those fabulous figures are a myriad of expenses, such as transportation, insurance, legal fees, arrangements, salaries, and taxes.

"The musician himself pays out of his own salary for uniforms, clothing, living expenses on the road as well as at home, upkeep of his instrument, and other personal expenses. The girl vocalist has plenty of expenses, too, considering all the formal dresses she must buy to keep looking her best for every performance."

**30 Evening Gowns**

Vocalist Helen Lee nodded her agreement, adding:

"I keep 30 evening gowns. Fifteen of them I keep with me on the road, while the other 15 are down in my hometown of Mobile, Ala., being cleaned."

Unlike many bands, the Jimmy Dorsey outfit does not have daily rehearsals. Each man in the band is an experienced musician, and does not need daily band practice to keep in top shape. The band rehearses only when the arranger brings in a new arrangement.

Personnel Manager Koerner describes the band this way:

"It's just like a professional football team. The band has a lead trumpet, lead trombone, and lead saxophonist who can be compared to the brilliant quarterback. And the rest of the musicians are like the sturdy linemen. The stars of the band are like the stars on a football team, and are paid accordingly."

**Trumpeter Teagarden**

Among the stars in Jimmy Dorsey's band are Trumpeter Charley Teagarden, brother of world-famous Trombonist Jack Teagarden, and Drummer Ray Badeuc. Badeuc was one of the original "Crosby Bobcats", exponents of Dixieland music who played with Der Bingle's brother, Bob.

No less a light is the renowned Jimmy Dorsey himself, one of the best on saxophone or clarinet. Born at Shenandoah, Pa., in 1904, Jimmy is the elder brother of equally-famous Tommy Dorsey.

The Dorsey brothers' father, a musician in his own right, taught Jimmy to play the clarinet and Tommy the trombone when they were still in short pants. Then, Jimmy recalls:

"While we were still in our 'teens we worked with local bands, and gradually made our way up to play under Paul Whiteman.

"After a few years with the King of Jazz, we formed the Dorsey Bros. orchestra. Then the feuding and other minor arguments that are common among brothers began, and we split up."

**Both Successful**

After the split, both Jimmy and Tommy became successful in the music world. Jimmy, for example, has made five movies, including one with his brother called "The Fabulous Dorseys," which took about six weeks to film.

Jimmy, however, readily admits that he prefers to be "on the road," or at his home in California, where he lives in a house built by Dick Powell.

"A cute little place of 11 rooms with a golf course and swimming pool," he describes it. He and Mrs. Dorsey have one child.

Most of the men in the band, like Jimmy, are married.

# CHAPTER 13
# ST. LOUIS BLUES

We did six shows a day for one week at the St. Louis Theater in St. Louis, Missouri. A 22-year-old, egocentric Mel Tormé ("The Velvet Fog") and the first "insult" comedian, Jack E. Leonard, were on the bill. At the 8 a.m. rehearsal, with Winfield conducting, the cocky Tormé kept putting down our band with such remarks as, "You call yourselves a name band? You can't even play in tune." I'm sure he wouldn't have pulled that crap if Dorsey had been present. Sure, hell — I'm positive!

Mel's big closer occurred when a drum set was wheeled out on the stage, and he would finish, to wild applause, with a frantic drum solo. Before the third show of the first day, Doc found several ten-penny nails and a hammer. He drove the nails into the housing of the bass drum, and bent them over all of Tormé's drum sticks. When the set was rolled out for the big climax, Mel hopped up on the drum stool, grabbed at his sticks, and couldn't extricate them to finish his act. Aha, pure intellect, and mature cunning and deceit had reigned! In tears, Mel apologized to each band member individually, and invited us to his hotel room for food and spirits after the last show. No one attended. So, there, Mel baby! Actually, Hoffman wanted to go up for a drink (more probably, *drinks*), but we wouldn't let him.

Leonard always came on stage wearing a hat with a wide brim. After a few jokes he would remove it and the audience would break up. A bald head will do it every time! He'd say, "What did you expect, feathers?" While the people were laughing at one of his jokes, he'd turn around and yell something dirty to the band. During applause, he loved yelling, "Hey, Bauduc, how's your cock and balls?"

I had dinner with Leonard one night between shows. We had soup, salad, entree and dessert. He finished his dessert while I was still toying with my entree. Jack then ordered another entire meal, and told the waitress to serve it in reverse. He consumed that one before I had finished my second cup of coffee. Leonard was quite obese, but I'm sure he went through that routine just to shock the other restaurant patrons, and to keep his image intact. Actually, he was a quiet, gentle man off stage, and we had a very pleasant conversation about his family and mine.

We always had trouble getting out through the stage door of the theater. Many young girls and older women would be waiting for Tormé and Dorsey. In order to prevent a riot scene, they both left by different exits. One frustrated little teener, unable to meet Mel, cornered me. She got my autograph, took my photograph, and vowed to start a fan club for me. How 'bout that! I took her to a drugstore for a soda, and sent her home. I received letters from 12 little girls for months after that. I answered them, too!

During that era, St. Louis was enmeshed in "blue laws." No booze could be sold on Sundays. Hell, for all I know, it was probably even against the law to play cards at home on that day. Everyone, including the band, just went across the state border to East St. Louis, Illinois on Sundays, where liquor and other "sinful" attractions were readily obtained. I'll never know what the St. Louis, Mo. city fathers expected to accomplish with their idiocy.

One night, after the fifth show, we were all sure Maynard wouldn't be able to hit the double high "E" on the end of *Rhapsody in Blue* for the last show. Ferguson's lips were a shambles. There was a blister on the large callous of his upper lip. Sure enough, he missed the "E" — and hit a higher "G." That cat wasn't human!

Another night, Charlie was very loaded. The stage was controlled by a hydraulic riser, and when it was raised, it presented a hell of drop to the pit. Teagarden had to side-step down from the trumpet section, and edge along the side of the bandstand to get up front for his featured Dixie spot. He negotiated it both ways, but when he got back to his chair, he moved it back as he sat down and fell off the rear of the stage! Dick and Joe just barely managed to reach back and grab him, and held him suspended while the rest of us finished the arrangement. Charlie was so fat they couldn't pull him up. Graves had a helluva time playing his trumpet left-handed while hanging on to Little T with his right hand. Many people in the audience stayed for the next show, thinking it was all part of the act!

**The author at the St. Louis Theater**

# CHAPTER 14
## THE FLYING EAGLE

We traveled by "The Flying Eagle Bus Lines," and we always had the same vehicle and driver — Charlie Mucci — another strange eye-talian! Most of us purchased winter caps at a sporting goods store when winter reared its ugly, frosty countenance. Mine was fur-lined, and sported ear flaps. (Of course, Bauduc bought a red tam and ear muffs!)

One day, Doc went up to the front of the bus and eyed Mucci's "Flying Eagle" shoulder patch for several minutes. The logo on the patch was of an eagle in flight. Clifford took out a pocket knife and began to cut and unravel the stitching on it. Mucci, helpless while driving, could only say, "Don't do that!!" Doc, referring to me, informed him that "The Eagle" had to have it. Florence sewed it on my hat that evening.

Dorsey usually rode in the Buick Roadmaster station wagon, with Romano driving. However, sometimes, if the band was grumbling about extra-long jumps, he would switch to the bus. Late one night, he had Mucci stop the bus across the highway from a road house, and left us there in the "Flying Eagle" to freeze for two hours. Later, we found out that he had been trysting with Martha Raye. We were not amused, and told him so in no uncertain terms. In a conciliatory move, he brought in a case of Dewars White Label Scotch the following night, and all was forgiven.

Whenever we passed through Langsford, PA., Mom Dorsey would sometimes hop aboard and tour with us for a while. She was a kick, and we didn't even have to clean up our language. I can still hear her say, "Holy Christ!" in her thick, Irish brogue.

Hoffman would consistently wander up and down the bus aisle doing the entire routines of comedians we had worked with. This got damned tiresome, as he'd keep doing the same act over and over until we backed a new comic. His favorite was a gag by Georgie Kaye: Man to psychiatrist: "Doctor, my brother eats grapes." Psychiatrist: "That's perfectly normal." Response: "Off the wallpaper?" Dick loved to yell, "Hey, I've got a two-dollar club date and a couple of small ones, if anyone's interested." This would prompt Artie to stick his head out the bus window and scream, "Georgette, Georgette, the werewolves are coming!" Waslohn would then awaken and say, "Robbick, robbick, I have a man in my throat!"

Aside from his inane comedic impersonations, Dick did have the foresight to take a camera with him on the road. Most of the photographs I have from these crazed times are copies of those that he took.

We never played cards or had jam sessions on the bus as portrayed by the Hollywood movie versions of the day. However, Stan Kenton's band once left their bus and paraded through some little town playing Sousa marches.

Once, Mimi directed Mucci off the highway and through the residential area of some dinky town in New Jersey. He finally found the house he was looking for, went inside, and returned with three, five-gallon jugs of homemade Dago Red — complete with sediment.

On another occasion, we pulled up in front of a restaurant in downtown Rochester, Minnesota. We careened out of the bus and into the eatery. Artie crawled in! Since the side of the bus was emblazoned with "Jimmy Dorsey, the World's Greatest Saxophonist, and His Orchestra," the pedestrians had no trouble identifying us. We completely fell apart when Winfield suggested that, as long as we were here, we might as well check into the Mayo Clinic.

# The Gang Around the "Flying Eagle" (Rochester, MN)

"Hangovers are swell"
Doc, Gene, Joe

"Here's how be-boppers smoke"
Joe Graves

"I've got a $2 club date
and a couple of small ones"
Dick Hoffman

Maxon, Masso, Graves, Mimi, Lolatte

"Everybody on the Bus!"
Lolatte and Hoffman

Bauduc, Hoffman, Graves, Lyons,
La Rocca, Bockey, Cenicola,
Maxon, Lolatte, Noble

# Boys On The Bus

**Teagarden, Romano**
**Winfield, Skippy**

**Doc and Mimi**

# CHAPTER 15
# DEAR OLD SOUTHLAND

Touring the South was a real experience. I had never been exposed to raw, brutal racial prejudice in Southern California, and the U.S. Army was segregated. We entered a town in Alabama that displayed a large banner hung diagonally across the main square. It proclaimed, "Nigger, don't let the sun shine on your head." Blacks could only come into town at night, and were not allowed on the sidewalk.

After checking in at our hotel, we asked one of the black porters directions to a good restaurant. A white man immediately confronted us, and asked, "Why are you talking to the nigra?" We explained, and the "good old boy" countered, "If you want to know something, ask one of us. Don't talk to the nigras."

The Southland was equally famous for its filthy diners. The cockroaches would scurry back and forth across the counters and practically fight you for your food — they really dug grease. Also, no matter whether you were having breakfast, lunch or dinner (even in the finest eateries), you invariably got grits and black-eyed peas with your meal — like it or not.

We performed in a converted storage garage in Dyersburg, Tennessee. The customers brought their own refreshments and sat at picnic tables. Larry went up to the mike for a vocal, and fell through the rotted planks of the stage. It was mandatory throughout the South to play their version of the National Anthem — *Dixie* — at the end of every engagement.

We played an unbelievably enormous tobacco warehouse in Fayetteville, North Carolina. People from all over the South attended. There was continuous dancing for three days and nights. The Les Brown and Harry James orchestras also participated, but we never saw them. People were bedded down in the hotel hallways, and you had to step over them to get to your room. "Moonshine" was abundant, and the dancers were always passing jugs and flasks up to the bandstand. That Southern "white lightning" was something else!

At the Folly Beach Pier on the Gulf near Charleston, South Carolina (George Gershwin wrote *Porgy & Bess* here), a terrible thunder and lightening storm passed over. It was too close for comfort for us. Noble (an ex-Marine, yet!) was so frightened he was unable to sing his vocals — especially since he spent most of the time under the piano.

We were relaxing at the pier's railing after the gig and the storm, when Joe Graves — morose, angry or whatever — suddenly reared back and threw his trumpet into the ocean. He then silently slunk back to the bus and went clear to the rear. (Only professional baseball players can relate to this type of behavior!) Somehow good old, obese Charlie T managed to waddle out into the surf and retrieve the horn. Thoroughly soaked, Charlie was the last one to board the bus. He went directly to the back and growled at Joe, "Here's your goddamned horn. Don't you ever do that again!"

We put in several days in and near the Mustin Beach Club and the Naval Air Base in Pensacola, Florida. For a week previous to this engagement, I was out of action with fever and stomach flu. Dorsey paid the doctor, my salary and Maynard's brother, Mike, who sat in for me. Damn nice! Florence Teagarden, a registered nurse, bathed me and gave me alcohol rubs. (Putting booze on the outside doesn't work as well, I found.) I returned to work on my birthday, shortly after Valentine's Day.

(In 1952, while I was playing with a small jazz group at the Hillcrest Hideaway in San Diego, a lady came up to me and said, "My husband has a photo of you in his den." Sure enough, the next night she brought in an 8x10 glossy of Dorsey's "Bop Group" front stage, with me and Maxon in the foreground, and Doc, Jimmy and Clare Hogan in the background. The back curtain had the same large Valentine's heart as the one in Pensacola. She gave me the picture.)

We reported for work to a locked arena in Louisville (Love-ull), Kentucky. Soon, the sidewalk was overrun with idiot union representatives, potential customers, curious onlookers and members of the press (more idiots). We were supposed to play there for two nights. Since we couldn't get into the hall, the local chapter of the Veterans of Foreign Wars invited us to their clubhouse for free food and 20-cent drinks. What an orgy!

During the festivities, I became enamored and elated when I managed to spirit what I thought (in my befuddled mind) was a gorgeous chick in a leopard coat away from the old pros, Doc and Mimi. Everyone razzed me the next day, and asked If I had enjoyed my evening with "that dog."

On the second night, Hoffman and I picked up a petite blonde and a chunky lady. Since Dick was partial to heavy women, everything started out on a high note (F, I believe!). We commandeered them to our room, using a bottle of whiskey and our animal maggotism as incentives. When I got around to nuzzling the blonde on the bed (she didn't seem to mind), the other lady became physically hostile. She turned out to be a bull-dyke, and accused me of making advances toward her lover girl. Although she still wanted to continue drinking our booze, Dick and I used our combined strength and managed to get the Amazon out of the room before we were seriously maimed. Unfortunately, the sylph went with her.

The heat and humidity were unbearable in Baton Rouge, Louisiana. It was 98 degrees in our hotel room at 4 a.m. Some of the guys went over to New Orleans (Nor-Lins) with Ray Bauduc (his hometown) the next day, but I was too wrung out to accompany them. I located a so-called "air-conditioned" cafe for breakfast. In those days, "air-conditioned" meant that they had a fan arrangement blowing air through ice water. It engendered a nice, clammy effect. When I walked out of the diner, the heat really slammed into me and I almost lost my breakfast.

BAND-LEADER Jimmy Dorsey and his orchestra showed up at the Armory last night for a dance concert, but found it all locked up. Armory Manager Irving Wayne said Dorsey wasn't supposed to play. Dorsey insists he was. He's showing a program to Joe C. Stone, head of the local Musicians Union. At extreme left is Gene Petrilli, a member of the local. Between Petrilli and Stone is Gilbert Koerner, Dorsey's manager. Helen Lee, the singer, and others in band stand before locked gates. Story on Page 9.

## Continuous Three-Day Southern Club Dance in Enormous Tobacco Warehouse

### Bands: Jimmy Dorsey Harry James Les Brown

**Mimi and Jimmy**

BALLROOMS were filled with fans who forgot about dancing and stood for hours to hear the incomparable Jimmy Dorsey

**Original "Dorseyland" Band**

# Jimmy Dorsey, Here to Play, Is Tuned Out

### Armory Says Contract With Band Never Made

Jimmy Dorsey and his band were all dressed up here last night—with no place to play.

Dorsey's manager, Gilbert Koerner, said the 15-piece ensemble and its two vocalists had a contract to give a concert-dance at the Armory.

Irvine Wayne, manager of the Armory, insists they didn't.

Caught in the middle were the would-be customers. Koerner estimated 100 of them appeared at the Armory and found just what the band did—locked gates. Some said they had seen advertisements of the show.

Wayne explained that the advertisements were put out as "feelers." He wanted to see if Dorsey had enough drawing power here to warrant an engagement, he explained.

**Claims No Contract Signed.**

The results of the ads showed, Wayne said, that "Jimmy doesn't have the drawing power his brother Tommy has." So, he said, no contract was signed.

While there was no actual contract, according to Koerner's understanding, there was something equivalent — a telegram from Wayne confirming the concert arrangements.

Wayne said no telegram of confirmation was sent. And as long as there's no signed contract and no deposit for the musicians' services, there's no contract, he feels. The deposit, he said, would have been $625, half of the proposed contract.

Dorsey himself had no explanation of the puzzle last night. He and Koerner both said that their booking agent, General Artists Corporation, knew more about the arrangements than they did. They said the agents had the disputed telegram.

**Musicians Union Peeved.**

Dorsey and his group arrived here Thursday night after a one-night stand in Evansville. They leave today for an engagement tonight in Cincinnati.

Though Dorsey just laughed when asked about the dispute, Joe C. Stone, president of A.F.L.-Musicians Mutual Protective Association, Local 11, was stern.

He said all A.F.L. musicians and associated artists probably will refuse to appear at the Armory unless Wayne fulfils payment of the Dorsey "contract."

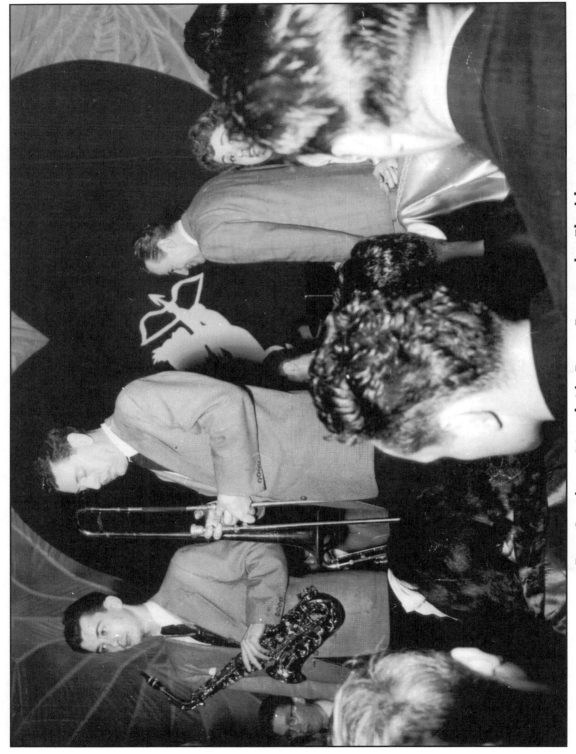

**Bop Section - Naval Air Base, Pensacola, Florida**
**(Maynard's shoulder, Gene, Chuck, Jimmy, Claire)**

# CHAPTER 16
## CORNVILLE

In the Midwest, we played Peony Park in Omaha, Nebraska. Ten of my Czech (Moravian) relatives showed up. However, since they were feuding, I had to visit two tables each intermission.

I stayed with my cousin, Nadine Ristau, in Fremont while we performed at the University of Nebraska in Lincoln. It was great to sleep in a real bed (duck down feather!) again. We had a genuine reunion with about 30 of my relatives at my Uncle Bill Walla's home, replete with an authentic Czech (Bohunk) feast. I ate so much pork spareribs, sauerkraut, dumplings and kolaches, I almost burst. We drank kümmel to wash all of it down.

We were at the Crystal Ballroom in Fargo, North Dakota in the dead of winter. The bus was parked in front of the ballroom, but I said to myself, "This is ridiculous. The Gardner Hotel is only two blocks away — I'll walk." I hadn't gone one block before the mucous in my nose froze. I was desperately looking for a St. Bernard before I made it to the hotel. When I got inside the immense, frontier-style lobby, everyone in town seemed to be lolling around the sizzling steam radiators. One old codger said, "It ain't too bad tonight — only 15 below." The wind-chill factor wasn't a consideration in those days.

### NEITHER SNOW NOR SLEET

We ran into a blinding blizzard on the way to Sioux City, Iowa. It got so bad we had to pull over to the side of the road for two hours. To make matters worse, the bus' heater went out. It was like being in the "Battle of the Bulge" again, except there were no critics shooting at us. We arrived at the ballroom three hours late to wonderful applause.

An article in *Downbeat* stated: "After battling the season's worst blizzard and cold wave thus far for nine hours with no rest or food, the Jimmy Dorsey band walked into the Tomba Ballroom and put on a wonderful performance. The crowd wasn't anything terrific, but considering that all roads leading into the city were practically impassable, the box office did all right."

Further down in the article, I got my first, though terse, mention in the publication: "In the reeds, Eugene Bockey stood out." Doc said, "That just means you played out of tune."

Dorsey was very drunk at the Frog Hop Ballroom in St. Joseph, Missouri. He played the entire four-hour dance with his coat pulled up over his head. We were so embarrassed, we all stayed sober!

While we were playing a one-nighter in Milwaukee, Wisconsin, we all had dinner at the famous Mader's German Restaurant. I earned a certificate by consuming two schweine schenkel (pork shanks), each weighing from two to two-and-one-quarter pounds. Actually, I couldn't quite finish the second one, but Doc conned the waiter into authenticating my gourmandism.

Four young ladies flirted with the sax section that evening. The greatest thing about being a sax player is that one gets to sit in the front row on the bandstand. I went to the YWCA with one of the girls after the dance. She took the elevator up to her room, and I tried to sneak up the stairs without the desk clerk seeing me. It didn't work, so we ended up necking in the lobby until it was time for the bus to leave. I told her we were going to appear for a month in the Ionian Room of the Deshler-Wallick Hotel in Columbus, Ohio (EH-HI-YA), and invited her to visit us.

Deutsche Küche       WHERE MILWAUKEE DINES

# Mader's German Restaurant
### 1041 NO. THIRD STREET     PHONE MARQUETTE 3377
### MILWAUKEE       WISCONSIN

### SOME OF OUR
### German Specialties
### YOU'LL ENJOY
●

Schweine Schenkel & Sauerkraut
Muenchner Kalbshaxen
Hammel Keule
Sauerbraten
Wiener Schnitzel
Schnitzel a la Holstein
Hungarian Beef Goulash
Szekelly Goulash
Koenigsberger Klops
Bayerische Leberkloesse
Leber & Blutwurst
Thueringer Bratwurst
Spanferkel
Hasenpfeffer
Ochsen
Sau
Kr
F
ash
n
ing
e
ackhuhn
t Turkey
Fish Dinners
Scallops
Oysters
Porter House Steaks
Beef Tenderloin Steaks

Established in 1914

## CERTIFICATE OF ACCOMPLISHMENT

KNOW ALL MEN BY THESE PRESENTS THAT *Gene Bockey*,
has successfully and meritoriously acquitted himself as appreciative of MADER'S GEMÜTLICHKEIT and reputation for good
food by eating TWO SCHWEINE SCHENKEL (Pork Shanks) and/or
gastronomical marvel, each weighing 2 to 2½ pounds; and in
recognition of said feat, and upon motion of the president,
this certificate is bestowed with beaming satisfaction upon
the holder hereof and said holder is entitled to the quaint
and rare honor of LIFE MEMBERSHIP in the great and glorious

### SUPREME COUNCIL OF PORK SHANK EPICURES

IN WITNESS WHEREOF we place our hands and affix the official
seal of the said council at the city of MILWAUKEE, all to
the honor of MADER'S glorified PORK SHANKS.

*George J. Mader*
President

*Gustave G. Mader*
Secretary

Witness *Chef Karl*

This ___ day of *January* 19__

Completely Air Conditioned

69

# Neither Snow Nor Rain . . .

Sioux City, Iowa—After battling the season's worst blizzard and cold wave thus far for nine hours with no rest or food, the new Jimmy Dorsey band walked into the Tomba ballroom and put on a wonderful performance.

The crowd wasn't anything terrific, but considering that all roads leading into the city practically were impassable, the box office did all right.

Dorsey and the band had the customers milling around the bandstand from start to finish. Not only were his dance arrangements well-received but the sidemen, old and new, provided a good show.

Charlie Teagarden and Maynard Ferguson, a youngster from Canada, in the trumpet section were outstanding, with the latter blowing the roof off. In the reeds, altoist Eugene Bockey stood out, and Ray Bauduc was tops on drums.

The band still had some one-niters left in the midwest before settling down at the Deshler-Wallick hotel in Columbus, Ohio.

# CHAPTER 17
# THE DESHLER-WALLICK

All four of the Milwaukee chicks were in front of the Deshler-Wallick's Ionian Room bandstand when we opened. I took my friend back to my room in the Virginia Hotel after the gig, and I'm sure Mimi, Doc and Artie did likewise with their "dates."

The girls didn't show up the next night, but a Columbus police detective did. He told Clifford that they had arrested four, 16-year-old Milwaukee runaway girls for shoplifting that day, and although he couldn't prove it, he knew our band was involved. There were four very nervous saxophone players that night.

My "jail bait" sweetie 'phoned the next morning and asked me to come down and bail her out of jail. I begged her to please not involve me, and to call her father. She called again the following day, asking me to come to the train station to see her off. Needless to say, I didn't make that gig!

On the way downstairs to the Ionian Room one evening, Doc and I were stopped by three young dollies. One of them asked, "Do you guys have any pot?" We had never heard marijuana referred to by that term before, and when the sweet, young thing explained, Doc said, "Get lost. We've had enough trouble with 'San Quentin Quail' like you this week!"

Columbus was the swingingest town, other than New York City, we'd been in. Everyone had at least one female "friend." Some of the guys even got involved with the "high-yellow" elevator operators and maids in our hotel.

There were four name bands working Columbus at the same time. Besides us, Charlie Barnet was out on Indian Lake, Charlie Spivak was in a local theater, and Stan Kenton was playing Ohio State University.

One night, after his last show at the theater, Spivak (an original member of the 1934 Dorsey Brothers band), fell by. He sat in on second trumpet and Dorsey played second tenor sax. Peter Lorre, the actor, came in. We all hovered around his table to view this sinister little man from *Casablanca* up close. He was an extremely shy man — not at all to be feared! But he sure could put away the booze!

Many cities had both "colored" and "white" musicians' unions in those days. The Columbus black local had a dance floor and bar upstairs in their hall, so we'd go there to jam after work.

The local announcer for our radio broadcasts, Bill Bramson, invited Larry Noble and me to the radio station to listen to transcriptions of some of our shows. He said he would make us copies of certain tunes for a price. Larry bought everything that had a vocal by him, but I only purchased *Aces Up* by our bop group. I sent it to my folks. My dad took it to a Mission Hills record shop where a high school girl friend of mine, Ruby Harding, worked. They couldn't play it because it had been recorded from the center out. Years later, I finally found an engineer who was able to transfer it to a tape.

While we were in Columbus, someone — I think it was Charlie — remembered that it was the band's first anniversary. He booked a banquet room upstairs in the Deshler, and had it set up with food and drinks after the job. When we got upstairs, our muscle man, Lolatte, immediately picked up Dorsey and carried him around the room in his arms, never putting him down for the duration of the party. Looking back, I suppose that was Bill's strange way of showing affection.

The second time we had a month at the Deshler, I met my future wife, Betty Lou Moon. We flirted as she danced by with her escort, and I kept mouthing the words (between notes), "Come to the tea dance tomorrow afternoon." She showed up the next day, and that was the beginning of a romance and a marriage that lasted 25 years. Since Doc was responsible for all of our nicknames, he designated Betty "The Owl" because of her enormous brown eyes.

Jimmy became progressively more loaded as the month went on. Toward the end, he began signing autographs, "Fuck you — Jimmy Dorsey." He was usually very sweet, but just couldn't cope with extended location jobs.

We were all invited to a ritzy home after work one night. Dorsey just sat in the corner playing the host's records. Every time he came across one by Artie Shaw, he broke it over his knee.

All of us were frequently asked for autographs, and we patiently complied. But sometimes, at Doc's instigation, we'd sign the names of other big band sidemen. One of our favorites was "Dave Matthews." Clifford's brain was always in gear.

In 1993, I talked to a San Diego trumpet player, George Lefebvre, who, as a teenager, came to the Ionian Room of the Deshler-Wallick to hear Maynard play. George has my autograph from that gig. (Déjà vu, all over again!)

**OPENING MONDAY!**

# JIMMY

(THE WORLD'S GREATEST SAXOPHONIST)

# DORSEY

## AND HIS ORCHESTRA

FEATURING LARRY NOBLE • HELEN LEE • RAY BAUDUC • BRAD GOWANS • CHARLIE TEAGARDEN

**DORSEY FOR DINING**
5:30 TO 8:00 PM (NO ENTERTAINMENT TAX)

**DORSEY FOR DANCING**
9:00 PM TO 1:00 AM

**JIMMY RAWLINS RHUMBA TIME**
Wednesdays at 11 PM, Ionian Room. Dance with the experts for prizes!

**ASTAIRE HOUR**
Fridays at 11 PM, Ionian Room. Learn from the Fred Astaire Dancers.

**"COCKTAILS AT THE DESHLER"**
Monday thru Friday, 5:15 to 6 PM, Ionian Room. Disc jockey program of music and quiz. Prizes. Transcribed nitely for WHKC 10:30 broadcast.

## THE IONIAN ROOM

*The Deshler*-WALLICK

**PALMER R. SUDDABY, GENERAL MANAGER**

## Around Columbus
### By Ben Hayes

**THIS BUSINESS** about Jimmy Dorsey fans being dog-eared—better get that straight right now.

Maynard Ferguson, the bop blower, shrills his horn until it becomes a silent dog whistle. He sails so high on the trumpet, goes the story, that only dog ears can hear him.

The Dorsey fans fill the Deshler's Ionian Room and their joy is apparent from ear to ear. But are those ears dog ears? Are they really hearing Ferguson? Or just pretending?

"They are hearing him," Dorsey said. "I hear every note he plays. Do I look dog-eared?"

I let that one go by, and turned to Johnny Davis, the Dorsey press agent, for more info about Ferguson.

The man with the high horn is from Montreal. He's only 20, but had a band of his own before joining Dorsey. Johnny said Ferguson plays a high E-flat note. He's one of three men in the entire country who can hit it.

And Dorsey is the man who can hear all three of them. He definitely is not dog-eared.

**HELEN LEE** (that's her real name) has red hair and brown eyes and Phi Beta Kappa brains. She's a belle from Mobile, Ala., adept at singing jazz and the blues. She wears evening gowns with straps and is not afraid of taking a deep breath. You can hear Helen.

Johnny Davis, the press agent, adores her. Johnny first saw Helen when they were students at the University of Alabama. In a show, Helen sang: "I Wanta Get Married."

"Oh, man, she knocked me out!" Johnny said. But he recovered, and married Helen. No children yet. Helen was named vocalist of the year by Pic. In college, music was but an elective. She led her class in art and science.

## Dorsey Will Not Go to the Dogs

Johnny, who grew up in Parkersburg just around the corner from Bill Slater (of Twenty Questions), attended Tulane and Michigan State, in addition to Alabama. He has a degree of criminology from Michigan State. During the war, he was a bomber pilot.

The Dorsey band is packed with interesting and talented people. Larry Noble, the male singer, is big and handsome, the tweedy type. He's from Hollywood and served in the Coast Guard with Victor Mature. He joined Dorsey last April, had been singing with Ted Weems.

Take one look and you know the drummer is Ray Bauduc, the dixielander who made the big noise from Winnetka. Charlie Teagarden, trumpet, is Jack's brother. The musicians talk much about the talent of the pianist, Al Waslohn. Dorsey's manager is Gil Koerner, who once sat down front playing saxaphone.

**MUSIC LOVERS** all over the country are hearing Dorsey from the Ionian Room. You'll enjoy seeing and hearing the broadcasts. WVKO and the Standard network bring in mikes at 7:30 p. m. nightly, and Saturday afternoons. It's Mutual 11:30 p. m. Tuesday and 6 p. m. Saturday. CBS carries Dorsey at 12:05 a. m. Monday through Friday. WELD also will carry Dorsey.

The four-week stay at the Deshler is making the Dorsey crew happy. Until they arrived here, They had been jumping everywhere throughout the midwest—Arkansas to the Dakotas.

"We learned by playing in all kinds of rooms that we've got it," Gil Koerner said. "Every crowd stayed to the very end—and we played before all kinds of crowds. We've got it."

**Dick, Gene, Charlie Spivak, Jimmy, Joe**
**Ionian Room, Deshler-Wallick Hotel, Columbus, Ohio**

Betty Lou Moon ("The Owl"), the future Mrs. Gene Bockemuehl

**Betty with Eddie Safranski
(Hal McIntyre Orchestra)
Latin Quarter - Boston**

*Gene Bockey alias Dave Matthews*

**The author, a.k.a. "Dave Matthews"**

**Gene**

**Betty**

**Eagle and Owl**

# CHAPTER 18
# THE MEADOWBROOK

From the time I was 14 years old I had listened to broadcasts from "Frank Dailey's Meadowbrook Ballroom — located on Route 23, just off the Pompton Turnpike in beautiful Cedar Grove, New Jersey." Sounds romantic, huh? What a letdown!

The Meadowbrook was a huge, barn-like structure, with a large dance floor and dinner seating for 2,000 people. The job hours were horrendous! We played dinner music from 7 to 8 p.m. and dance tunes from 9:30 to 2:30 a.m. On Saturdays, we had to play "Matinee at The Meadowbrook" from noon until 1:30 p.m. There was no town there (or to quote Gertrude Stein, "there was no there there") to speak of, so we were forced to buy expensive meal tickets from Dailey and eat on the mezzanine so we wouldn't disturb the "real people." We commuted every day from the President Hotel in New York — quite a distance — and we were there for a month. Judging by his generosity (?) and short (?) working hours, one would never had guessed that Dailey was an ex-bandleader!

We had two coast-to-coast radio broadcasts every night, and three on Saturdays. Charlie Barnet must have heard one of them because he stole Ferguson from us. Of course, Kenton shortly thereafter stole Maynard from Barnet, so I guess all's fair in love and war and big bands!

On an off night, Jimmy took some of us to hear Barnet's band (with Maynard) at the Clique Club (later called "Birdland") on Broadway in New York City. Jimmy, who was feeling no pain (as usual), went right up to Charlie and said, "Charles, the band sounds as ponderous as ever." Barnet broke up. It was a wild band. This was the lineup: trumpets — Johnny Howell, Ray Wetzel, Doc Severinsen, Rolf Ericson and Maynard Ferguson; trombones — Ken Martlock, Dick Kenny and Billy Burgess; saxes — Danny Bank, Kurt Bloom, Vinnie Dean, Reuben Leon and Dick Hafer; piano — Claude Williamson; bass — Eddie Safranski; drums — Cliff Leeman; conga — Carlos Vidal; singers — Chuck Clark and Trudy Richards. It was a good thing the club was a concert venue, because no one would have ever been able to dance to Barnet's charts!

During the '60s, I ran into Charlie in the bar of the Kona Kai Club on the bay in San Diego where he lived on his yacht. I reminded him of that night, and Charlie said, "Jimmy was right. Those bastards sure were ponderous." We drank and talked about

81

the good old days until closing. The bartender put a fresh bottle of Dewars on the bar and went home. Barnet and I consumed most of it while we ran down The Beatles and all the other rock groups until 6 a.m., whereupon Charlie turned off the lights, locked up the joint and wove his way down the wharf to find his boat. I drove the ten miles through Mission Valley against day-gig traffic to my home in Allied Gardens with one eye closed!

Back to The Meadowbrook ..... One Saturday morning, Doc, who lived at #1 Christopher Street in New York's Greenwich Village, decided to drive his brand new 1949 Chevy to Cedar Grove — to hell with the bus. Larry and I decided to accompany him. Also, we were to pick up Dick at his home in West New York, New Jersey.

We were already behind schedule when we found Dick's place, and from then on the trip was a complete disaster. We couldn't find the Meadowbrook! Everyone we asked sent us in a different direction.

Totally frustrated, Clifford finally turned on the radio, and we listened to "our" broadcast — minus first and second alto, male vocalist and lead trumpet.

We arrived at the ballroom to a chilly reception, to say the least. Doc explained what had happened, but we sure weren't looking forward to the evening's performance. Charlie had played "lead" and did all the male vocals on trumpet, and Jimmy had played lead alto. Everyone steered clear of us.

For my solo, during the night broadcast, Jimmy announced me as "Husk O'Hare." I later received a letter from my father in which he said, "We finally picked up one of your radio shows, but didn't hear you play. A fellow named "Husk" played an alto solo that was quite good, though."

The first Lenny Bruce-type comedian, Lord Buckley, was on our show the opening week. He was hilarious, extremely dirty, way over the diners' heads, and resplendent in his hip, all-suede suit. At rehearsal, he ran us through all kinds of music, coached Bauduc on innumerable breaks and sound effects, and then announced, "By the way, I don't use any music in my act." You never knew what he was going to do. His act was entirely different every night.

One evening, he persuaded eight people to sit in a row on the dance floor, and he stood behind them. He told them that every time he touched the back of their heads, they were to move their mouths. He then proceeded to do a 15-minute, risque "Amos 'n' Andy" program.

The comedian B.S. Pulley also did a week. His opening remark to the audience was, "Ladies and gentlemen, you probably wonder what the "B.S." stands for. It stands for "bull shit!" That was pretty racy for the '40s. Both comics entertained us in the bandroom every intermission with much filthier, and to us, funnier material. Buckley always had "musician" stories for us. He told one about Red Rodney "blowing" a horse on the Steel Pier in Atlantic City. Every night after that, whenever Red would go out to the ballroom, the horse would neigh longingly at him.

Honest, Red — we knew it wasn't a true story!

**Good old ex-bandleader Frank Dailey's club on
Route 23 of the Pompton Turnpike in Cedar Grove, New Jersey**
(At least B.S. Pulley and Lord Buckley were on the show)

7 p.m. - 8 p.m. - Dinner Music
9:30 p.m. - 2:30 a.m. - Dancing
Every night --
plus
"Matinee at Meadowbrook"
noon - 1:30 p.m.
Every Saturday

# CHAPTER 19
# ANOTHER JUNE, ANOTHER TUNE

Doc took his new Chevy on the next road trip. Artie and I rode with him. Going through Cicero, Illinois, which was right outside of Chicago and just as corrupt, a cop stopped us. Doc tried to hand him a $20 bill. The indignant protector of the law said, "Don't do that! Drop it on the ground!" Clifford complied, and we went merrily on our way.

Lyons turned in his notice in Kingston, New York. He had decided to join Doc Evans' small jazz band in Chicago. Jimmy was furious. After the job, Dorsey asked Clifford if he could ride with him to the next town, not knowing that Artie was going along. We drove all the way to Syracuse with a sullen, mute Dorsey. The rest of us were afraid to break the silence.

Meanwhile, back on the bus: upon entering Kansas City, Missouri, we went past the Hotel Muehlebach. Waslohn turned to me and said, "Eagle, you've got to become a band leader. Just imagine the marquee — Bockemuehl at the Muehlebach."

We were booked into the Surf Club in Virginia Beach, Virginia — a wide-open gambling spot — for two weeks. Many of the guys lost their shirts playing roulette in the casinos. My "hip" mirrored sunglasses came into my possession due to Clare Hogan's luck at gambling — she needed five dollars!

The first week in Virginia Beach was a joke. It rained like hell, but the management insisted that we work outside. Although the bandstand was protected by a roof, the dancers weren't; consequently, no dancers. The club's major-domos relented the second week, and brought us inside. We filled the joint. You figure out that marketing strategy! Virginia Beach had weird liquor laws. The customers brought their own booze, but had to buy "set-ups" (soda, orange juice, ice, etc.) from the house.

In Minneapolis we played a one-nighter at the Corn Palace. What a bizarre looking building — inside and out! Dorsey took the whole band to a restaurant in a small Negro district in St. Paul after work. Talk about a really "one-of-the-guys" leader! At that time, there were probably less than a couple hundred blacks in the entire Twin Cities area. The owner-chef was an old friend of Jimmy's. Dorsey had been coming to this eatery since the early '30s. The owner brought us heaping plates of brick-oven barbequed ribs and coffee cups filled with whiskey. What a feast!

We crossed paths with Dick Strickland's "territory" band. They showed us their "sleeper" bus — three tiers of damn Army cots slung on each side. They never checked into hotels, and made $75-$85 a week. But, come to think of it, they weren't very good musicians, either.

The whole band cheered en masse when our bus rolled past Young's Rubber Company in Trenton, New Jersey. After all, that was the outfit that manufactured Trojan condoms!

Late one night in Pennsylvania, I glanced out of the bus window and saw what looked like an enormous, wrinkled white sheet hung on a clothes line strung across the sky. I woke Artie and exclaimed, "Am going nuts? What the hell is that?! He answered, matter-of factly, "Those are the Northern Lights, Eagle — one seldom sees them this far south."

Dorsey received word that his home had partially burned down, and his wife had been severely injured. Good old Ben, the butler, had carried Jane out of the house. Jimmy immediately flew to the coast, and we had four days off. I took a train to Columbus, and stayed with Betty and her mother in their apartment.

After sitting on the grass in a park in Columbus (near Cleveland and Myrtle streets) most of one day, my feet and ankles swelled to enormous proportions that evening. A doctor came to the apartment and told me I had been bitten by "chiggers," and that their poison and the dye from my socks had caused the swelling.

Back in Manhattan, I drew lots of attention while walking down Broadway in my powder blue suit, wearing Betty's mother's bright red house slippers.

**Back on the Bus**

## HOTEL MUEHLEBACH COFFEE SHOP

**"Bockemuehl at the Muehlebach"**

| | | | | |
|---|---|---|---|---|
| MADE IN U.S.A. | | | NUMBER 7110 | |
| EARNINGS AND DEDUCTIONS FOR PERIOD ENDING | | | | |
| July 26 | | | 19 49 | |
| EMPLOYEES NAME | E. Bockey | | | |
| SOCIAL SEC. NO. | | | | |

| | | | | |
|---|---|---|---|---|
| YOUR TOTAL EARNINGS ARE | | | 245 | 82 |
| DEDUCTIONS ARE AS FOLLOWS: | | | | |
| FOR OLD AGE BENEFITS | | | | |
| UNEMPLOYMENT INS. | | | | |
| WITHHOLDING TAX | | | 35 | 35 |
| WAR BONDS | | | | |
| FOR Suit | | | 36 | 10 |
| FOR | | | | |
| FOR | | | | |
| FOR | | | | |
| YOUR TOTAL DEDUCTIONS | | | 71 | 45 |
| YOUR NET PAY | | | 174 | 37 |

EMPLOYER

**(includes recording date)**

## Wife of Bandleader Burned in Blaze

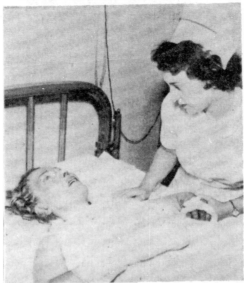

Mrs. Jane Dorsey, wife of Jimmy Dorsey, bandleader, is shown in St. Joseph's Hospital in North Hollywood after she sustained first, second and third-degree burns as flames damaged the Dorsey home early yesterday. With her is Nurse Carmen Powers. (A.P. Wirephoto.)

## JD Rejoins Band; Wife Recovering

Hollywood — Jimmy Dorsey rejoined his band in the east after hurrying out here to see his wife who was badly burned when the Dorsey home in North Hollywood was damaged by fire recently.

Mrs. Dorsey is in St. Joseph's hospital where she is recovering. Ben Murphy, Dorsey household aid, who carried the leader's wife to safety, was credited with saving her life.

The house was so badly damaged that it is practically uninhabitable. Dorsey said he was not yet certain whether it could be repaired and that it was not possible to estimate the loss except that it might run as high as $50,000, including a valuable record library.

## Jimmy Dorsey's Home Razed; Wife Burned

HOLLYWOOD, Feb. 21 (UP)— Fire swept through bandleader Jimmy Dorsey's palatial Lakeside home today and severely burned his wife.

Mrs. Dorsey, 39, dragged from her room in the fiercely burning home, was in serious condition with burns on the face, hands and chest.

The $125,000 home was destroyed. The loss included Dorsey's irreplaceable collection of records and musical arrangements.

## Mrs. Dorsey Seriously Hurt

HOLLYWOOD, Feb. 21 (UP)— Mrs. Jane Dorsey, wife of Bandleader Jimmy Dorsey, was in serious condition tonight from burns she suffered when her palatial home near San Fernando Valley caught fire.

The Dorsey butler, old-time Actor Ben Murphy, and his wife, Victoria, dragged Mrs. Dorsey to safety but not before she suffered burns on her face, hands and chest.

**MANSION DAMAGED**

The fire broke out early today in one wing of the $125,000 mansion, completely destroying it and damaging the rest of the house. It took six engine companies to put out the fire. The cause was not determined pending an investigation.

Mrs. Dorsey's screams awakened the Murphys in servant quarters adjacent to the main building. They rushed to the house and dragged Mrs. Dorsey from her flaming bed.

**SEDATIVES GIVEN**

A neighbor, Dr. Carl Lund, gave Mrs. Dorsey first aid and sedatives as she was taken to an emergency hospital. Later she was transferred to St. Joseph's Hospital.

The saxophone-playing Dorsey was out of town on a tour of the South with the band. The Dorseys bought the rambling home several years ago from Actor Dick Powell. Mrs. Dorsey is the former Jane Porter, a one-time dancer.

# CHAPTER 20
# THE HOTEL PENNSYLVANIA

Needless to say, the success of big bands first came via radio, and then from recordings. We have the astute management of the Hotel Pennsylvania in New York City to thank for the first remote radio pickup in 1921. The maestro would announce into the mike, "Lopez speaking." During the '40s, every dancer in America knew the hotel's telephone number through Glenn Miller's hit recording of *Pennsylvania 6-5000*.

Since we were going to play Manhattan for at least a month, Gil informed us that the Musicians Union (Local 802) had insisted that out-of-towners deposit their union cards with them until we left. Mimi took to me to union headquarters.

There were ten (count 'em, ten!) surly, black business agents glowering at us from behind wire-mesh windows. (In San Diego, we had one business agent who was usually half-asleep!) After my transaction was finished, Mimi took me downstairs to the hiring hall. The contractors were standing like slave traders on small platforms in this immense room, and the potential sidemen were jockeying around trying to get a gig for the night. There must have been 300 people in the room — all hungry for work!

When we went back on one-nighters, I went to the union to pick up my card. A less-than-amiable union rep said, "Your engagement was over the day before yesterday. Youse guys didn't pick up your cards, so we mailed them back to your locals." God, how I love pompous union officials!

Opening night of our month-long stay in the Cafe Rouge of the Hotel Pennsylvania (Statler) in Manhattan was memorable. Columnist Michael Levin, writing in *Downbeat*, summed it up thusly: "Highlight of the evening was when Tommy Dorsey wandered in, was introduced to the crowd by Jimmy as 'Homer Rodeheaver,' and got off groaning chunks of '*I Love You Truly*' while the band played '*Darktown Strutters' Ball*.' Not to be outdone, Jimmy took apart his clarinet, and played feeling Teschemacher clarinet, to be shortly joined by the brothers' mother, who danced a few bars on the stand. All is indeed well in the Dorsey household."

Actually, Jimmy was always very proud about being able to emulate the word "s-c-r-e-w" with his clarinet on occasions such as this.

After an intermission of table-hopping, Dorsey informed me that a lady who went to San Diego High and San Diego State with me was in the audience. I went over to her table during the next intermission and was invited to join the party. Her name was Harriet Van Natta, but as a New York model, she had changed it to Honey Hilton. During the conversation, and unrelated to anything we had been talking about, a man said, "You know, with your widow's peak hairline, you'll lose your hair before you're 40." I figured him for Honey's date, so I just answered, "Really?" After just coming off a slew of horrendous one-nighters, who wanted to start a confrontation with an idiot? (To paraphrase an anonymous quote, "I consistently refuse to engage in a battle of wits with an unarmed opponent!" I'm now 71 years old, have all my hair, and it's still black—with just a touch of "mature gray" at the temples!)

Honey had been two grades behind me in high school, but I remember drooling over her, from a distance, in the college lunch room after the war. A romance developed. She was 5'10" tall, and insisted on wearing three-inch heels. We made quite a pair since I stood all of 5'8-3/4"!

She had a great apartment somewhere in the East Forties, and I'd often go there after work. When she gave parties, I'd be the bartender (never get too far away from the booze!). She was always giving me presents (monogrammed hankies, inscribed cigarette case, etc.), and only wanted horse and carriage rides through Central Park in return. A rich friend of hers once invited a party of 12 of us to the Latin Quarter for drinks, dinner and the floor show. Even in those days, that must have cost a bundle.

One night, I sheepishly told her I wouldn't be able to see her for a while since another woman (future wife, Betty) was due in town to visit. She took it quite well, probably thinking it would soon blow over, and that she and I would eventually marry. Honey even called me in San Diego after I had left the band to invite me to her parents' home on Pershing Drive (classy neighborhood). I didn't go. I never saw her again — a major mistake I'm not proud to admit to.

Hoffman was in heaven at the Hotel Pennsylvania. Every intermission, he'd high-tail out a side door, cut across the street to "Kelly's" and get his fix of three Manhattans and a beer chaser. One of us would give him the high-sign to scurry back for the next set.

Ray Anthony and his wife were in several times to dance. I'm sure "Agony" was there just to steal ideas. Another band leader, Les Brown, would also bring his lovely wife in for dancing. Jimmy knew tempos, and our band was always danceable.

At one point, Dorsey was incapacitated (drying out in his room) for four days. I played the theme song, *Contrasts*, just like Jimmy on our nightly broadcasts, and Charlie conducted and played Dorsey's solos. Bobby Hackett took Teagarden's place in the trumpet section. I don't think the radio audience at home knew the difference.

One day we had to come in early. A Selmer Musical Instrument Company photographer was there to take pictures of the Selmer users in the band. Mimi and Dick borrowed Selmers so they could get into the photos. Selmer ran them in a full-page ad in *Downbeat* and *Metronome*. The Harry James orchestra was also featured in the spread. My old Bonham Band director, Jules Jacques, was delighted because two of his band alumni — Nick Buono (trumpet with James), and myself — were featured.

Betty came to the city, and we discovered New York together. We'd cavort on the roof of the Flat Iron Building, ride on the Staten Island Ferry, visit the Empire State Building, roam through Central Park and take the subway (five cents) to Brooklyn. (For some reason, we never visited the Statue of Liberty.) On the way home from work, I'd buy a bottle of B&G Sauterne and get two, take-out dinners at the Mexican restaurant across the street from the President Hotel. We often went to a cellar club in Greenwich Village that only served wine. It was a large room furnished with couches and coffee tables. We'd order a bottle of B&G and be entertained by a gay, black ventriloquist.

Knowing my admiration for the music of Claude Debussy, Bill Kraft invited Betty and me to sit in the control room of a radio station in Times Square while an entire symphony string section broadcast the great composer's string quartet in the studio. What a wonderful recording that would have made!

Members of "The Jimmy Dorsey Aggravation" (also known as "The Dorsey Dervish") would often head for "Charlie's Tavern," a famous musician's hangout, after work. It was a meeting place and contact spot to get gigs. Contractors would often 'phone there to find out who was available. Also, every third drink was on the house — which, in itself, was an incentive to hang around.

Mimi and I went in one night and were invited back to the kitchen to sniff heroin. (No, not cocaine!) Mimi went in, but I continued to guzzle alky at the bar. I'm glad I didn't participate, because I'm sure I would have loved it. I've had some problems with alcohol in later life, but thank God, I never was a junkie.

"Mattress Annie" arrived!  Every sideman in New York (and throughout the country) was aware of that infamous groupie.  There are still as many "Mattress Annie" stories circulating among old jazz musicians as there are those about Joe Venuti.  At least half of them are really true — about both of those characters.  If Annie had been around in the next musical era, Elvis would have been put away long before he built Graceland!

Johnny Dankworth, the esteemed British reed man and husband of vocalist Cleo Laine, dropped by the Cafe Rouge one evening.  He cornered the sax section and said, "You gentlemen get an exceptionally good blend, especially when Mr. Dorsey augments it to six sax-often-ists."  From then on, whenever somebody asked one of us what instrument we played, the answer was, "I'm a sax-often-ist."

One Night Stand With **JIMMY DORSEY** Cafe Rouge, New York

MAR. 28, 1949

JOYCE LP—1048

# *One Night Stand With*

# JIMMY DORSEY
## *Cafe Rouge, New York*

### MARCH 28, 1949

**JOYCE LP—1048**

**SIDE ONE**

1. THIS CAN'T BE LOVE
2. HERE I'LL STAY (Vocal by Larry Noble)
3. SEE SAW (Arranged by Neal Hefti) (ME) (SHORT SOLO)
4. GREEN EYES (Vocal by Larry Noble and Claire Hogan)
5. SING A SONG OF SIXPENCE
6. I CAN'T GET STARTED
   (Vocal and trumpet by Charlie Teagarden)
7. A LITTLE BIRD TOLD ME
   (Vocal by Claire Hogan)

**SIDE TWO**

1. BODY AND SOUL (Featuring Maynard Ferguson)
2. DIZ DUZ EVERYTHING (ME) (LONG SOLO)
   *Hollywood Palladium, Summer 1947*
3. MY HEART IS A HOBO (Vocal by Skylarks)
4. LOVE'S GOT ME IN A LAZY MOOD
   (Vocal by Dee Parker)
5. EASY TO LOVE (Vocal by Bill Lawrence)
6. PARADE OF THE MILK BOTTLE CAPS
   (Arranged by Pat McCarthy)

CHUCK MAXON

*Personnel for March, 1949:*
Charlie Teagarden, Dick Hoffman, Maynard Ferguson, Dick Murphy (tp) Herb Windfield, Jr., Al Corraine, Dick Bellerose (tb) Jimmy Dorsey (cl/as) Doc Clifford, Gene Bockey (as) Frank Mayne, Phil Cenicola (ts) Mimi LaRocca (bar) Al Waslohn (p) Carl Kress (g) Bill Lolatte (b) Ray Bauduc (d)

*Personnel for 1947 broadcast:*
Bob Alexy, Irv Goodman, Cy Baker, Shorty Solomson (tp) Frank Mancusi, Bob Alexander, Sonny Lee, Don Matteson (tb) Jimmy Dorsey (cl/as) Bill Covey, Kenny Dehlin (as) Chuck Travis, Jimmy Giuffre (ts) Danny Bank (bar/fl) Bob Carter (p) Steve Jordan (g) Barney Spieler (b) Karl Kiffeld (d)

Personnel supplied by Tom Cullen who is currently working on a Jimmy Dorsey discography which should be ready for publicat on late 1978.

*JOYCE MUSIC is publishing a complete line of Big Band Discographies. Each book contains all the commercial recordings made by the band, along with personnel, dates, locations, master numbers, and record numbers (including reissues on LPs). Also listed are transcriptions, movie work and any radio or TV programs known to be preserved. Indexes of tune titles are a part of each book. These books are soft bound, printed on 8½ x 11 paper and a complete collection of these should be a part of every serious collector's library.*

*Available books include Charlie Barnet, Jan Savitt, Larry Clinton, Elliot Lawrence, Tony Pastor, Hal McIntyre, Buddy Rich, Tex Beneke, Charlie Spivak, Bob Chester/Teddy Powell, Les Brown, Artie Shaw, Harry James 1937-1950, Harry James 1951-1975, Claude Thornhill and Cab Calloway. More will be forthcoming in the near future. Ask your local jazz dealer for these books. If they are not available, write*

*JOYCE MUSIC CORPORATION*
*Box 1707, Zephyrhills, Florida 33599*

JOYCE MUSIC CORPORATION
Box 1707
ZEPHYRHILLS, FL 33599

JOYCE

## By Michael Levin

New York—Jimmy Dorsey opened here at the Hotel Statler (formerly yclept Pennsylvania) last month to the plaudits of a trade crowd which spent its evening remembering similar Dorsey events over the past 14 years in this town.

Highlight of the evening was when Tommy Dorsey wandered in, was introduced to the crowd by Jimmy as "Homer Rodeheaver," and got off groaning chunks of *I Love You Truly* while the band played *Darktown Strutters Ball*. Not to be outdone, Jimmy took apart his clarinet, and played feeling Teschemacher clarinet, to be shortly joined by the brothers' mother, who danced a few bars on the stand. All is indeed well in the Dorsey household.

Things were not quite as well with the band itself. Drummer Ray

**Mike**

Bauduc played an uneasy combination of two and four-beat music all evening long, seemed at home only behind the *Muskrat Ramble* which Tommy led on trombone. Trumpet Charlie Teagarden's work was largely subordinated to the playing of 20-year-old Marshall Ferguson, who, while fast technically, has the typical James "nanny" tone and tends to throw too many scales into his solos.

Jimmy stated frankly from the stand that the band was evenly divided between the bop and Dixie influences. Certainly both solo styles were demonstrated, though at no time did really convincing music ensue.

**A great deal of the slightly humdrum, colorless presentation may have resulted from the killing road tour the band has just come off.**

Certainly everyone in the outfit was yearning to sleep and not to play.

In view of past Dorsey triumphs, particularly since he is so well-liked as a leader and a person, it will be nice to see him make a good showing at what was practically his home during the band's peak days of 1941-42.

He is completely sincere about combining bop and Dixie. Even Bauduc seems to be making motions towards picking up on various of the bop elements. If it works out, it will be a wonderful tribute to JD's ability as a leader, but, at this writing, nothing more than interested expectancy can be reported.

# Café Rouge
# Pennsylvania Hotel
# New York

Claire Hogan, featured vocalist with Jimmy Dorsey's band at the *Café Rouge*.

Jimmy Dorsey, with the best band he has ever had, has come back to town to stay for a while. Except for a one night engagement, last October, at a Broadway ballroom, his music hasn't been heard in New York dance spots for about two years. Now, he is making up for that long absence, in the Hotel Statler's beautiful Cafe Rouge. He is on the bandstand there, nightly except Sunday.

With the band are a pair of vocalists—Larry Noble and Claire Hogan—who have been attracting enthusiastic attention on tour. Like Dorsey's instrumentalists, most of whom are from Hollywood recording studios, these singers are tops. And by and large, judges of music are saying the aggregation adds up to the great band which Dorsey has always vowed he would produce.

Honey

Gene

For Honey A. Lion

Latin Quarter Party - New York City

# On two continents, leading players agree...
## You'll Play Better With a Selmer

The world's highest-paid players all know that, with a Selmer, you realize your fullest musical capabilities. When *you* play a Selmer, you give your musicianship its greatest range ... on an instrument identical with those played by artists pictured on this page, and many others. Try a Selmer at your dealer's today. You'll play *better*.

HENRI SELMER PARIS

**HARRY JAMES** has played a Selmer (Paris) Trumpet for 12 years. SELMER ARTISTS in James' band: **back**, Bob Poland, Nick Buona, James, Bob Walters, Corky Corcoran; **front**, Pinky Savitt, Willie Smith, Sam Sachelle.

► **JIMMY DORSEY**, ace saxophonist and leader, is a Selmer (Paris) player. His Selmer artists: Mimi La Rocca, Gene Bockey, Maynard Ferguson, Dorsey, Dick Hofmann, Arty Lyons, Phil Cenicola, James "Doc" Clifford.

◄ **THREE GREAT FRENCH ARTISTS**, all on the faculty of the world-famed Paris Conservatory, play Selmer (Paris) Instruments: l. to r., Marcel Mule, Raymond Sabarich, Ulysse Delecluse. These men cooperate in the development of Selmer improvements.

H. & A. Selmer INC.
ELKHART, INDIANA

SELMER, Dept. A-71, Elkhart, Indiana

Without obligation, send your free booklet on Selmer (Paris) Instruments.

Name.................................Instr...........

Street........................................

City.................Zone.....State.........

**AVAILABLE AT BETTER MUSIC DEALERS EVERYWHERE**

# CHAPTER 21
# SALARIES AND RECORDING DATES

When I had been with the band for six months, I received a raise to $135 a week. Dorsey paid lead men, married men and "stars" more money. I'm sure Doc, Charlie and Ray were in the $200-250 range, and Maynard made just a little more that I did. When I left the band, I was up to $150 per week, and recording and transcription dates were icing on the cake.

In the beginning, we couldn't record commercially. A recording ban was in effect due to the dumb domination of James Caesar Petrillo, president and czar of the International Musicians' Union. However, we did have several dates with Atlas and Standard Transcriptions. These recordings were distributed to radio station disc jockeys, but were not sold over the counter to the general public.

The sessions were recorded either in the middle of the night after our New York gigs, or at 8 a.m., and would last as long as six hours. We'd use our best jazz material, with very few vocals. These were usually done in old St. Patrick's Cathedral because of its three-story ceiling. This was prior to the advent of stereo, but we got a great echo effect because of the superb acoustics in the church.

We usually made between $100 and $150 per session in addition to our regular salaries. If we had two or three of these a month, the money would really add up. I sent either a $50 or $75 money order home every week. When you're doing one-nighters, it's almost impossible to find someplace to throw money around. (When I returned to San Diego in 1949, I had over $7,000 in the bank, which was a lot of cash in those days. A nice home in San Diego could be had for around $9,000.)

We started recording for Columbia Records when the ban was lifted. Alan Reuss, the great section guitarist, was added for the dates. God, how he swung the band! We cut two sides on the first date, after our job at the Cafe Rouge. The first one featured Larry Noble on a typical ballad, *Here I'll Stay*, and it went off like clockwork in two takes. The second was a can of worms. Clare "Shanty" Hogan had to sing idiotic, tongue-twisting lyrics to a forgettable up-tempo piece of crap called *Fiddle-Dee-Dee*. It took 22 trials before we got a passable master. Hogan's screwing up of the lyrics and the band's 3 a.m. less than wide-eyed nonchalance were the causes for this disaster. Since this was before the introduction of tape, there could be no mistakes (no splicing) from beginning to end.  If this particular 78 rpm side is played on a modern stereo set, Doc and I can be faintly heard yelling "Fuck," when we were supposed to be background singing, "Fiddle ......!"  Find it, and you've got a real collector's item!

On our next date, we cut a wonderfully fast *Sweet Georgia Brown*, featuring Jimmy, backed by *Kiss Me*, a clever novelty featuring Hogan and Charlie.

While I was working the "4 Girls 4" show (Rosemary Clooney, Helen O'Connell, Rosemarie and Margaret Whiting) at the Fox Theater in San Diego in 1978, a young trumpet player said to me, "I've just been to Tower Records, and they have three Jimmy Dorsey LPs with your name on the back of the jacket."  I raced to that record emporium between shows, and was able to pick them up.  They were re-recorded live broadcasts of the 1948-49 band.  Two tunes, *Diz Does Everything* and *Seesaw*, featured Maynard, Chuck Maxon and me.  What a gas!

# JIMMY DORSEY
## AND HIS ORCHESTRA
*featuring*
# MAYNARD FERGUSON
## "DIZ DOES EVERYTHING"

### SIDE ONE

1 DIZ DOES EVERYTHING . *ME* .......................... 4:50
2 BIG BUTTER AND EGG MAN .......................... 2:05
3 ALWAYS TRUE TO YOU IN MY FASHION .......................... 4:15
   vocal by Claire Hogan
4 LET'S FALL IN LOVE .......................... 3:07
5 SEE SAW . *ME* .......................... 2:06
6 I CAN'T GET STARTED WITH YOU .......................... 3:55
   vocal by Charlie Teagarden
7 NEVERTHELESS .......................... 3:09

Personnel:

Jimmy Dorsey: Leader, Alto Sax and Clarinet on all sides
TRUMPETS: Maynard Ferguson, Charlie Teagarden, Dick Hoffman,
   Dick Murphy
TROMBONES: Herd Windfield, Al Lorraine, Dick Bellerose
SAXOPHONES: James Clifford, Gene Bockey, Frank Maynes, Phil Cenicola,
   Mimi Laroca
PIANO: Al Washlon
GUITAR: Nappy Lamare
BASS: Bill Lolatte
DRUMS: Ray Bauduc

### SIDE TWO

1 THIS CAN'T BE LOVE .......................... 2:49
2 MELANGE .... *AL. WASLOHN* .......................... 3:03
3 ALTO-TUDE .......................... 2:46
4 McGEE'S CLOSET .......................... 3:49
5 BODY AND SOUL ... *MAYNARD* .......................... 4:43
6 A LITTLE BIRD TOLD ME .......................... 3:05
   vocal by Claire Hogan
7 SING A SONG OF SIXPENCE .......................... 2:58

THE EXACT DATES OF THESE BROADCASTS ARE UNKNOWN BUT PROB-
ABLY SOMETIME BETWEEN MARCH AND MAY OF 1949. NO COM-
MERCIAL RECORDINGS WERE MADE OF THIS PARTICULAR BAND
FEATURING THE GREAT TRUMPET WORK OF BOTH MAYNARD FER-
GUSON AND CHARLIE TEAGARDEN.

Maynard

100

# CHAPTER 22
# THE PARAMOUNT

We were booked into Manhattan's famous Paramount Theater — the Mecca for big bands in the "Big Apple." On the bill with us were Peggy Lee, backed by husband Dave Barbour's small group, the comedian Georgie Kaye, and the great black dance team, Tip, Tap and Toe. The movie for the first four weeks was *The Great Gatsby* starring Alan Ladd; a forgettable flick, *Desert Sand*, with Lizabeth Scott, bombed for the last two weeks of our gig. We did six shows a day for six weeks, with Mondays off. Our first show was at 11:04 a.m., and the last ended at 12:22 a.m. the next morning. We drew 10,000 people on opening day.

The band would congregate in the basement while the "trailers" (cartoons, short subjects and news) were on. After these, the stage would rise to about halfway up in front of the screen. Dorsey would ding you with a $25 fine if you missed the raising.

Between shows, we would usually go to a nearby Irish saloon to down martinis and smoke gage. When we got back on stage, we'd never have to move our somewhat paralyzed heads. We could see Jimmy start and stop the group by watching the large mirror in the back of the theater, and we had the music memorized. During some intermissions, Dave Barbour's drummer, Alvin Stoller, and I would go several floors upstairs and play vibe and alto duets.

Actually, we could get a "contact high" on marijuana by merely passing by Tip, Tap and Toe's dressing room on the way to our own. No wonder their routine was different every performance!

Tommy Dorsey and Benny Goodman showed up in the basement one morning. Jimmy borrowed three trumpets, and they proceeded to play Herbert L. Clarke trumpet trios in harmony until it was time for the stage to go up. We were awe-struck!

During the last show one night, Mimi and I made eye contact with (and waved at) two chicks in the front row. We met them out in front of the theater after the gig. My date turned out to be Glynis Johns, the British film actress who was in the U.S. to make Disney movies.

Mimi craftily steered the girls to the bar in the President Hotel, where I had a room. They wouldn't drink. In anger, Mimi finally said, "Shit, let's go up to Gene's room and smoke some dope." Damned if they didn't acquiesce! As soon as we lit up, Glynis said, "This stuff is terrible. Try some of mine." She took a mascara container from her purse, opened it, and extracted three joints. We ended up in Glynis' Park Avenue apartment.

I had also dated two other film actresses: Evelyn Keyes (Scarlett O'Hara's younger sister in *Gone With the Wind*, who later married John Houston and Artie Shaw — but not at the same time), and Anne Jefferies, who, with husband Robert Sterling, starred in the Topper TV series in the '50s.

My mother forwarded me a letter from the Veterans Administration. It stated that If I didn't return to college that fall, I would lose my GI benefits. As a disabled veteran, I was paid $200 a month while attending school under Public Law 16, with tuition, books and other supplies paid for by the government. I decided I had better take advantage of this.

Jimmy was always hurt and angry whenever someone quit his band, and would sometimes not speak to them while they worked out their two-week's notice. I gave notice to Gil Koerner who tried to talk me into waiting until we got to Omaha again, so my train fare wouldn't cost me as much. I'm sure he thought he could talk me out of quitting before we got that far. Finally, in desperation, he said, "Jimmy wants to talk to you."

I girded my loins and headed for the confrontation in Dorsey's dressing room. When I entered and sat down, he quietly said, "Big bands, as we know them, are on a down-slide and will eventually disappear. If you're not doing this because of an involvement with a woman, you've made the right decision."

I left the band in August, 1949.

Paramount Theater - New York City - 1949

Paramount Theater - Sax Section Featuring "Cymbal-Minded" Gene

Paramount Theater - Brass Section

808 ROCKNY O'N. 7-11    1-2 01
Jimmy Dorsey Orch **HOTEL PRESIDENT**
N° 11 40    148TH STREET WEST OF BROADWAY
NEW YORK 19, N.Y.

| | | DATE | EXPLANATION | | AMT. CHARGED | AMT. CREDITED | BAL. DUE |
|---|---|---|---|---|---|---|---|
| | 1 | JUL11-49 | ROOM ●●●● | ★ | 3.00 | | |
| | 2 | JUL11-49 | MISC ●●●● TAX | ★ | 0.15 | | ★ 3.15 |
| | 3 | | | | | | |
| | 4 | JUL12-49 | ROOM ●●●● | ★ | 3.00 | | |
| | 5 | JUL12-49 | MISC ●●●● TAX | ★ | 0.1— | | ★ 6.30 |
| | 6 | JUL13-49 | ROOM ●●●● | ★ | 3.00 | | |
| | 7 | JUL13-49 | MISC ●●●● TAX | ★ | 0.1— | | ★ 9.45 |
| | 8 | JUL14-49 | ROOM ●●●● | ★ | 3.00 | | |
| | 9 | JUL14-49 | PHONE ●●●● | ★ | 0.12 | | |
| | 10 | JUL14-49 | MISC ●●●● TAX | ★ | 0.15 | | ★ 12.72 |
| | 11 | JUL15-49 | ROOM ●●●● | ★ | 3.00 | | |
| | 12 | JUL15-49 | PHONE ●●●● | ★ | 0.12 | | |
| | 13 | JUL15-49 | MISC ●●●● TAX | ★ | 0.15 | | ★ 15.99 |
| | 14 | JUL16-49 | ROOM ●●●● | ★ | 3.00 | | |
| | 15 | JUL16-49 | MISC TAX | ★ | 0.15 | | ★ 19.14 |
| | 16 | JUL17-49 | ROOM | | 3.00 | | |
| | 17 | JUL17-49 | MISC TAX | ★ | 0.15 | | 22.29 |

**One week's hotel bill!**

| DATE EFFECTIVE | July 16, 1949 | **PROGRAM** | THEATRE | Paramount |
|---|---|---|---|---|
| DOORS OPEN | 9:00 A. M. | AND **SCHEDULE** | CITY | New York |

| LENGTH OF RUN | 1st Week | ~~#BEGINNING AND DATE#~~ Saturday - Only | ~~#CLOSING AND DATE#~~ Open: Wed. 7-13-49 |
|---|---|---|---|

### TIME SCHEDULE OF SHOWS BY UNITS

| UNIT AND TITLE OF PROGRAM | RUNNING TIME | 1ST SHOW | 2ND SHOW | 3RD SHOW | 4TH SHOW | 5TH SHOW | 6TH SHOW | 7TH SHOW | 8TH SHOW | 9TH SHOW |
|---|---|---|---|---|---|---|---|---|---|---|
| Advance Trailers | 4 | | 11:00 | 1:37 | 4:14 | 6:54 | 9:36 | 12:18 | | |
| UNIT: JIMMY DORSEY & BAND | 55 | → | 11:04 | 1:41 | 4:18 | 6:58 | 9:40 | 12:22 ← | | |
| Intermission | 5 | | 11:57 | 2:34 | 5:11 | 7:51 (7) | 10:33 (7) | - - | | |
| FEATURE: "THE GREAT GATSBY" | 91 | 9:25 | 12:02 | 2:39 | 5:16 | 7:58 | 10:40 | 1:15 | | |
| Intermission | 3 | - - | - - | - - | 6:47 | 9:29 | 12:11 | 2:46 | (OUT) | |
| Paramount News | 4 | 10:56 | 1:33 | 4:10 | 6:50 | 9:32 | 12:14 | | | |
| | | | | | | | | | | |
| | | | | | | | | | | |
| In Person: Peggy LEE-Jimmy DORSEY & Band-Dave BARBOUR & Quintet-Georgie KAYE-TIP, TAP & TOE | | | | | | | | | | |

**New York - Paramount Theater**
**Six shows a day - 11:00A.M. - 1:00A.M.**

**Peggy Lee, Dave Barbour, Georgie Kaye, Tip, Tap and Toe, Jimmy Dorsey Band**
**Movie: "The Great Gatsby," with Alan Ladd**

106

# Sidemen Switches

Jimmy Dorsey replaced altoist Gene Bockey with Nino Palotti. . . Tenor man Preston Hudson with Bob Chester, replacing Buddy Arnold. . . Glen Gray substituted Lou McCrary, trombonist, for Russ Sonjou.

Trumpeter Dale Fitzmorris left Jimmy Featherstone to join Shep Fields. Bill Freese replaced. . . Mario Daone, trombone, took over Gene Steinman's chair with Benny Goodman. . . Chris Cross added trumpet man Ernie Englund.

# CHAPTER 23
# POST-DORSEY
# (CODA)

In 1952, The Jimmy Dorsey Orchestra came to Tops' Restaurant on Pacific Coast Highway in San Diego for a week. The guys stayed in seashore cottages in Ocean Beach, and had a ball. Phil Cenicola and Bill Lolatte were still with the band, and Artie Lyons and Doc Clifford had re-enlisted for the Western trip. Jimmy was going to disband and merge with brother Tommy after their Las Vegas engagement. Doc, Phil and Bill planned to establish residences in Vegas, and Artie wanted to get back to the Los Angeles area. A fine young bop trombonist, Frank Rehak, had joined the band, and Shorty Sherock had taken over Little T's chair.

When I walked into Tops', Doc handed me his alto, and disappeared. I think Jimmy was surprised at my reading ability and sound on lead clarinet on the long, symphonic introduction to *Laura*. I took a jazz solo on some tune, and the guys told me I had changed my style. Doc thought I sounded like Lee Konitz. I told them that I was just out of practice.

I took Bill, Artie and Frank to some local jazz clubs to play on Sunday afternoon. Everyone was knocked out by Rehak's playing. The guys told me that I had to come up to Hollywood. They were booked into the Hollywood Palladium, and there was going to be a Jimmy Dorsey reunion party at some club. I had just graduated from college, so Betty and I made the trip.

Helen O'Connell and I sat in with the band at the Palladium. Jane Dorsey was there, and of course, the asshole — Mickey Rooney — showed up. Some nights I sat in with Jack Teagarden's little band at a club on Hollywood Boulevard. Joe Graves and Ray Bauduc were with the group, and "Bumps" Myers played tenor and clarinet. He used a wire coat hanger for a sax strap. Errol Garner was the intermission pianist.

An entire night club on La Cienega Boulevard was taken over from 2 p.m. until 2 a.m. for the reunion. Hundreds of musicians showed up. Betty and I circulated, but spent most of the time at a table with Maynard and his new bride, starlet Kay Brown. Otherwise, all I remember is that someone repeatedly spilled sticky Stingers on my new, custom-made suit, and Betty and I had to rescue Helen O'Connell from an amorous Dorsey in the parking lot.

The Dorsey brothers were re-united in 1953. Jimmy would lead the band for the first few sets, featuring his own arrangements. Tommy would then come on stage, and take over for the rest of the evening. Tommy was the boss. Lee Castle, a trumpet player, was assistant conductor and acted as the line of communication between the brothers.

An old pal of the boys, Jackie Gleason, chose the Dorseys as the 1955-56 summer replacement for his TV show, and they (not Ed Sullivan, as is commonly thought) had the dubious distinction of introducing Elvis Presley to the viewing public. If that doesn't make the brothers turn over in their graves, nothing will!

The band appeared in a beach community between San Diego and Los Angeles, so Betty and I drove up to see them. Jimmy handed me his alto, and I played some blues, and for the last time rendered Jimmy's theme, *Contrasts*. Tommy said, "You play the brother better than he does, but he plays you better than you do." Touché!

Tommy, Jimmy, Betty and I had drinks after the dance. Tommy had coffee. He had been on the wagon for a few years. We went out to the parking lot, and Tommy proudly showed us the bus and trailer truck he had purchased. He said, "Now, not only do I do my own booking, but I don't have to depend on some stale shit-heel to provide transportation." That was Tommy — always aggressive and profane.

And that was the last time I saw either one of the Dorsey brothers.

\* \* \*

On November 26, 1956, seven days after his 51st birthday, Tommy choked on some food in his sleep, and died at his home in Greenwich, Connecticut. Jimmy, inconsolable, tried to carry on. He died six months later, on June 12, 1957, of lung cancer in a New York hospital. He was 53. Only a few days before, Lee Castle had presented Jimmy with his gold record for *So Rare*, which had sold over a million copies. That was probably the last gold record earned by a big band.

I continued in the music business through 1961, finishing up with five years in Jack McLean's "Mickey Mouse" band at the Mississippi Room of the Manor Hotel on El Cajon Boulevard in San Diego, and playing with the San Diego Symphony Orchestra . I'm retired now, after teaching band and orchestra in the San Diego City School System for 20 years.

**NEW YORK** — The Dorseys made music and magic. And thanks to the miracle of electronics, their wondrous sounds have an enduring quality. Un-

**Dorsey**

like his firecracker brother, Jimmy Dorsey was easy going, soft - spoken and a dedicated musician. Last year, Jimmy spurned an opportunity to perform a solo on a teevee show. His brother later explained: "Jimmy is a perfectionist. He doesn't play anything unless he can do it backwards first." During their personal wars, Tommy retained the deepest respect for his brother's musical ability. "There isn't anyone," he once said, "who can hold my brother's horn. He can play anyone off a bandstand." When Glenn Miller heard that comment he remarked prophetically: "Some day those two guys will get back together. Blood is thicker than swing."

No wonder the original Dorsey band had the nation swinging and dancing. In addition to Tommy and Jimmy, it included a youngster playing second trombone and arranging named Glenn Miller. On the trumpets were Bunny Berigan and Charlie Spivak. Ray MacKinley was on the drums and vocalist was Bob Crosby. The Dorsey legacy is priceless: Beautiful music and warm memories.

# Jimmy Dorsey Dies In N.Y. Hospital     1957

NEW YORK, June 12 (UP) —Orchestra leader Jimmy Dorsey died today of lung cancer, still grieving over the death of his trombonist brother, Tommy, six months ago.

Jimmy, 53, died in Doctor's Hospital at 9:30 a.m. He had been a patient there three months. His closest friend and associate said Jimmy apparently died without knowing he had cancer.

"He used to say, 'Get me my clothes, I'm going home'," when I went to the hospital to see him," the friend, Lee Castle, said. Castle told reporters he is going to keep the old Dorsey band going.

Dorsey was told when he underwent an operation last Jan. 3 that he had a wart on his lung. He thought nothing about it, because that is a minor affliction common among musicians, Castle said.

Jimmy last appeared four months ago in the Roseland ballroom here with the band he and his brother formed after they ended a feud that lasted more than 10 years. He directed the orchestra in the playing of his famous theme song, "Contrast" and an old song back at the top of the hit parade—"So Rare."

That was after his operation. When it came time to go on tour with the band, Jimmy was unable to make the trip. He returned to the hospital, never to leave it again. The band is playing at the Hotel Statler.

Tommy Dorsey choked to death in his sleep at his Greenwich, Conn., home Nov. 26.

"Since Tommy died, Jimmy hadn't been the same," Castle said. "He cried night after night. He was broken hearted. I think his sorrow must have speeded the end."

By 1989, Jimmy and Tommy, Jack and Charlie Teagarden, Al Waslohn, Artie Lyons, Brad Gowans, Ray Bauduc and Doc Clifford — and maybe more of the guys — had passed away. Most of them died while in their early 50s.

That same year, Lolatte, Cenicola and Hoffman were residing in Las Vegas. Bill in real estate, Phil with Nat Brandwynne's "house band" in various hotel-casinos, and Dick as a musical director. George Masso was — and still is — a sought-after player at jazz festivals, plays with "The World's Greatest Jazz Band," and in 1985 was the trombone "voice" for actor Wayne Rogers in the movie, *The Gig.* Joe Graves was fronting the Harry James Band; Lee Castle was touring with his version of the Jimmy Dorsey Band; and Maynard Ferguson is now fronting a jazz-rock-fusion "Big Bop Nouveau Band" (ugh!).

In 1993, I called Phil in Las Vegas, but his son said he couldn't speak on the 'phone as he was an Alzheimer patient, aged 80.

* * *

At this writing, I am 71 years old. I started to play again after a 15-year hiatus of wearing false teeth (because of progressive gum disease caused from not brushing my teeth for six straight months during combat). My son, Eric, deserves the credit for my return to playing. He turned me on to "Fixodent," a denture adhesive that really works! The technique came back (mostly) in just a few months, but the chops and inventions seem to be taking a bit longer.

**ADDENDUM**

## Doc's First Letter

One Christopher Street
New York 14, New York
November 1st, 1949

Dear Eugene:

Well, I,too, finally gave up with JD. We had an anniversary "party" at Mc Keesport - the Vogue Terrace- to celebrate the first year of the band, so I added my bit to the festivities by giving notice. Today, technically, is my last day, but at the request of the management, I'm "helping out" till they get a satisfactory replacement. That consists of a record date tomorrow and three one-nighters - Thur.,Fri.,and Sat.; I sure hope they have someone by then 'cause now that I've taken the step I'm very anxious to get all the way out. I guess you can appreciate that feeling.

Things went on in much the same gruesome fashion after you left. The Canadian trip was wilder than any of the preceding ones. Everyone, JD very much included, seemed to be trying to act out the ginger ale ad. Joe Graves announced his "marriage", he took that weird-looking blonde chick with him on the bus. Somewhere enroute she allegedly became pregnant. He and Stubby were fired right before we opened the Statler. I saw Graves last night - he told me they were getting a divorce - HAH!!! He also said that he was selling sponges, for his Florida relatives, to the larger department stores. That's one of the many stories he has told of his activities around town. He gets stranger every day. One of the trumpet replacements was fired at the Statler and Shorty Sherock came on. What a curious one he is!!! He carves Graves at the SAG routine - out-Mc Koys Clyde - puts on a false nose and plays an, sure as death, original polka which rapidly segues to "The Stars andStripes Forever" with the whole band marching around the dance floor. You'd have to see it. He also does a routine with the old man which consists of their cackling at each other while they scrape their feet on the floor. They have an argument during which they say very funny things with the horns - Dorsey naturally gets to say "scccrrrewww" quite a bit, then they make up. They've been doing this on all the jobs, even in theatres. It's excruiatingly comical.

Noble also got fired just before the Statler. He really flipped- went around muttering imprecations and making all sorts of dire threats for days. He later got to the they'll-be-sorry-when-I'm- big-star stage. What an idiot !

Waslohn gave notice the same time I did. He's been scuffling with Hogan like mad. She's now making it with JD. Honest to God! I know it's probably hard for you to believe, but it's a fact. You should see the way she comes on now. Al made a real jerk of himself. I never believed that he was that serious about her, but he made it obvious in front of the whole band.

JD was his usual self at the Statler, he got progressively more loaded every night, and, finally, the night before we closed, he didn't show up at all. It was the same style as before, we did the broadcasts without him and Teagarden fronted the band. He,

113

incidentally, is still on the wagon. He looks very good, and he's really blowing up a storm. He dropped an awful lot of weight. We're wondering how long it will last.

I'm starting to work with Miguelito Valdez next Monday. The band is at the Havana-Madrid and they have two television shows. I hate that kind of music, but I'll make exactly the same money as with Dorsey - and they stay right here in NY. A couple of my old chums are with Valdez - Jack Schwartz and George Berg. At least I'll be out of my mind all the time.

The Dixieland band has a record date today. They're doing eight sides. They got Dick Cary and Cutty Cutshall in place of Waslohn and Winfield, otherwise the lineup is the same including Lolatte. Was he ever surprised!! Winfield is really sore - he was very fractured in Charlie's last night and was doing an act like Noble.

I saw Ferguson yesterday - Barnet broke up after their date at the Apollo - he's probably going with Shaw. Some deal about fronting the band when Shaw takes off for concert dates. He's thinner than ever and brother Mike is quite fat. Mom and Pop still are with him, and they still have the same Ford with 1948 license plates.

Maxon is still acting cool, and requesting "Aces Up" every night. He's wearing one of JD's cast-off overcoats and is the official driver of the Cadillac for which detail he is supposedly being paid $50 a week. Bauduc is still getting hell every night, and is lousing things up as usual. Phil is worse than ever - JD has convinced him that he can't play flute - as a result he has quit about twice a week. Koerner talks him out of it - he knows that if Phil goes he'll have to go back to playing that chair. Mimi stays out of his head as always, and he's about ready to pack it in. The guy who took your place is a real mamma's boy - he worries all the time - and is in a big hurry to get to the end of whatever tune we play -- what with Bauduc's slowing things and his rushing -- very interesting ! The tenor-man is a staunch Youall - he's from Charlotte, N.C., and he's due for a visit from AA almost any day; the same goes for the first trombone. Hofmann is relying more and more on Manhattans with a beer chaser, and he won't let us up with Georgie Kaye's material.

This is about it, Eugene, if you get a chance drop me a line. Regards to Humph if you see him or hear from him. Take it easy.

Doc

114

## Doc's Second Letter

1 Christopher St. NYC 14
May 16th, 1950

Dear Gene:

It's been a long time since I wrote, but there are extenuating circumstances; I should have said have been ex etc. As you no doubt heard I
didn't go with Valdez, instead I joined the show band at the Copa. I was
doing a lot of other work besides, and as a net result wound up in bed
for three months. The medical term; spontaneous pnuemothorax --- the
King's: a collapsed right lung. It didn't give me any pain except in the
ass. You can't do anything except stay in bed. But for WQXR and WNYC, the
stations here that play music, I would have flipped worse. I haven't
gone near the TV, nor cracked a book since. I've been up about six weeks,
and working about four.  I now do 3 nights at the Copa - MonTueWed- and
if any one calls me for the weekend - great- if not- the frau and I make
for Penna. MahHome!! This collapsed lung deal is not as serious as it
sounds. There are no after-effects, it's as tho' it never happened; and,
at my doctor's behest I've gone back to all my usual habits - bad and
otherwise.

The latest on the JD "aggravation" (Lolatte's word for it)
Koerner got the axe last week - has been replaced by John Hall from
Sammy Kaye. Roy Hamerslag, the erstwhile Insurance nuisance, replaced
Hall with the Kaye org. I was talking to John the day it happened; he
said that no money had been turned in to the office in over a month, also
that the books were so fouled-up it would take some time to find out just
what was happening. The Koerner System of Quadruple Entry Bookkeeping.
GK is supposedly in town - has been seen around Charlie's - I haven't
come across him as yet. I'm more than anxious to hear his no doubt
apocryphal version of it all. One of the first things Hall plans is to
unload Gibeling; he has a decided antipathy toward both Howard's writing
and his personality. I had a note from Lolatte saying that there was wild
rejoicing and dancing in the streets when the band heard the news. VK day
has taken it's place in history along with VE and VJ days.

When I was first up and about I stopped by the Statler to see the guys;
everything was much the same as when we first graced the stand there--
JD was fractured -- LA Rocca was staring wildly at everything in skirts -
Phil had just ordered another flute made of cadmium-plated uranium or
somesuch and I injured him by asking why didn't he learn to play the one
he already owned -- Hoffman was still woodypeckering over to Kelley's
for Manhattans with beer chasers - UGHHH!!! The skinny CT - no toper, he.
The inventor of the Maxophone had received his Dishonorable --Winfield
had huffily left under the stigma of a Section 8 -- Waslohn had rejoined
but was in the process of disjoining(he recently got married -- his
childhood flame from Oil City -- she's quite zoftic - to us Aryans, that's
buxom -- probably spelled wrong anyhow -- he's now accompanying Claire
"Shanty" !!!!! Hogan, who's doing a single at a joint on the Island (Long)
by name The Queen's Terrace -- she's recently recorded for London ---
Anent all this: Oh what a tangled web we weave when first we  --- you
finish it!!!) To get back to the Statler: Bauduc was still sitting behind,
playing ahead and behind, and just generally being a horse's behind; I've
concluded that he spends his time compounding interest on his doubtless
numerous bank accounts --- Low-life was still as large as and looking
more like the Italian Johnnie Weismuller than ever -- That's all of the
group that's left -- OOPS !! NEW SHeet

Have you and the Moon went and done it yet? Or have you been maintaining the status quo ante, or what?

The Valdez group had a balling time in Puerto Rico -- I'm now sorry that I didn't go -- probably would have avoided the spontaneous etc. or at most would have completed the deal -- how many guns does a T/5 rate?

I'm now mulling over several gigs for the summer -- I'll undoubtedly latch onto the wrong one, but the sun is the same no matter where. The NEW SOUND groups are all heading for the Jewish Alps(Catskills) while the JEFF DAVIS contingent has taken over the Jersey shore. Of course the MamboBoys -- Whassamatter you can no play in clave? -- have taken over the best jobs in each sector. I'll probably wind up in the Alps; although one of the Rhumba cats came up with a good deal yesterday. At any rate it has to be settled before next week.

A friend of yours from Dago called while I was in the last stages of convalescence in Penna. --- by name, I think, Joe Bird -- when I got back he had left the President, they knew from nothing there. Sorry I missed him.

I got a 50 Chevvy last week -- much like the 49 only a different color-- yellow-- and Power Glide, which means no clutch etc. -- A pretty groovy vehicle -- I sold the 49, after putting 26000 on it,to the cop on the corner here -- I'm still holding my breath.

Eleanor and I have been talking about making a move out of NY sometime within the next year or so; we've thought of Miami,Phoenix, Tucson, Vegas, the Coast; we're definitely going to do something, but when or where ??? Do you know anything about Vegas, or Arizona?

I saw in the Beat where Humphrey had made some records with a Chicago group -- Doc Evans -- Dear Humphrey - I wonder where he is tonight -- his atavistic tendencies have probably come to the fore and he is a werewolf leaping over Chicago roof tops. I shall certainly never forget my driving you and Humph to Syracuse with the sulky, sullen JD in the front seat.

John Hall, before he left to join the Dervish, asked if I'd be interested in doing the Paramount with same. There's a new union rule which requires an all 802 band in the Broadway theatres. If I don't hie myself off to sunnier parts I probably will do. I'll keep you posted.

This is it for now, dear boy; write when you get a chance.

Your loving uncle,

Doc

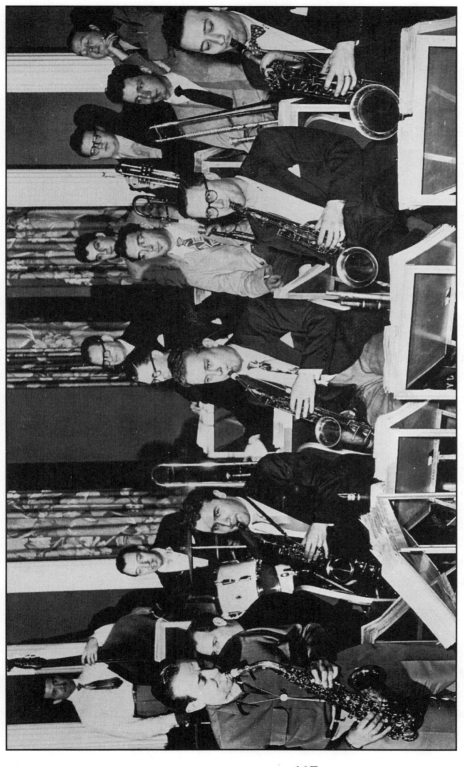

## Jimmy Dorsey Band - 1950

**3rd Row:** Bill Lollate, Charlie Teagarden, Dick Hoffman, Dick Murphy, Shorty Sherock
**2nd Row:** Ray Bauduc, Bob Hackman, Dick Belrose, Frank Rehak
**Front Row:** Jimmy, Frank Maynes, Nino Palotti, Benny Fussell, Phil Cenicola, Mimi La Rocca
Not shown: Pianist Dick Cary

**D**ixie 1950

dorseylanders carey at piano, bassist lolatte,
clarinetist JD, trombonist hackman, tenorman mayne,
trumpeter teagarden, drummer bauduc

One band that has been heard often and which is credited
in many spots with being the major force in the revival of
Dixieland is Jimmy Dorsey's. It's records are a mixture of quite
good Dixieland and some pretty forced stuff. The band plays
some good two-beat instrumentals, with Charlie Teagarden, Ray
Bauduc and Dick Carey the most legitim... of its purveyors of
this form of jazz. But you'll also hear some strict novelties that
feature Claire Hogan singing half in a Helen O'Connell manner and half in something which we suppose is novel Dixieland. The small Dorseyland group has been backing her with
obvious lack of enthusiasm, not because Claire can't sing but
because she and they are both so restrained by a formula that
has apparently been instigated by a desire not to make good
jazz but to make much moola.

# SAMPLE ITINERARY

## (October 14, 1948 to August 2, 1949)

I've endeavored here to indicate, through the piecing together of old itineraries, my last road trip with "The Jimmy Dorsey Aggravation." The date is followed by the location, the venue, and the hotel we called home for that period. Where I could, I've shown the mileage (in parentheses) between successive gigs.

<u>1948</u>
### October

14 - NYC, Standard Transcription date; Hotel Belvedere
15 - North Adams, MA, Armory; Richman Hotel
16 - Lewiston, ME, Arena; Lafayette Hotel (Portland, ME)
17 - Holyoke, MA, Valley Arena; Roger Smith Hotel
18 - Montreal, Canada, Danceland; Laurentian Hotel
19 - open for travel
20 - open; Forrest Hotel, NYC
21 - Mahoney City, PA
22 - Philadelphia, PA, University of Pennsylvania
23 - Washington, D.C., Uline Arena
24 - Bridgeport, CT, Ritz Ballroom; Barnum Hotel
25 - Danbury, CT, Armory
26-30 - Wrenthem, MA, King Phillip Ballroom; Stage Coach Inn
31 - open for travel

### November

1-7 - Geneva, NY, Club 86; Seneca Hotel
8 - open for travel
9 - Peterborough, Canada, Palace Pier; Ford Hotel (Toronto)
10 - Toronto, Canada, Arena; Ford Hotel; (mileage 95)
11 - Niagara Falls, Canada, Arena; Ford Hotel (mileage 90)
12 - London, Ontario, Canada; Arena; London Hotel (mileage 130)
13 - Detroit, MI, Armory; leave after job
14 - Cleveland, OH, Castle Farms; leave after job
15 - open
16 - Murray, KY, College Auditorium
17 - Evansville, IN, Vendome Hotel (mileage 150)

18-19 - Louisville, KY, Arena; Brown Hotel
20 - Cincinnati, OH, Castle Farms
21 - Newark, OH, Theater; Warden Hotel (mileage 175)
22-27 - McKeesport, PA, Vogue Terrace; Alpine Hotel
28 - open for travel
29 - Appleton, WI
30 - Kaukana, WI, Nightingale Ballroom; Valley Inn

## December

1 - Rochester, MN; Auditorium; Zumbro Hotel
2 - Marion, IA, Armor Ballroom; Montrose Hotel (mileage 190)
3 - Lincoln, NE, University of Nebraska; Lincoln Hotel (mileage 300)
4 - St. Joseph, MO, Frog Hop Ballroom; Robidoux Hotel (mileage 180)
5 - Sioux City, IA, Tomba Ballroom; Warrior Hotel (mileage 260)
6 - open
7 - Sioux Falls, SD, Arkota Ballroom; Carpenter Hotel (mileage 90)
8 - open for travel
9 - Pittsburg, KS, Tower Ballroom; Besse Hotel (mileage 550)
10 - Fayetteville, AR, University of Arkansas; Mountain Inn (mileage 150)
11- Kansas City, MO, Pla-Mor Ballroom; Continental Hotel (mileage 250)
12 - Omaha, NE, Peony Park (mileage 211)
13 - open
14 - Montevideo, MN, Gladys Ballroom; Hunt Hotel (mileage 311)
15 - Mankato, MN (mileage 136)
16 - Fargo, ND, Crystal Ballroom; Gardner Hotel (mileage 309)
17 - St. Paul, MN, Prom Ballroom (mileage 260)
18 - Waterloo, IA, Electric Park (mileage 196)
19 - Clear Lake, IA, Surf Ballroom (mileage 90)
20 - open
21-23 - Madison, WI, Orpheum Theater; Lorraine Hotel
24-26 - Indianapolis, IN, Indiana Roof; Lincoln Hotel
27 - Dyersburg, TN
28-30 - Chicago, IL, Croyden Hotel
31 - Rockford, IL, Armory

**1949**

**January**

1 - Milwaukee, WI

2 - open, Columbus, OH ; Virginia Hotel

3-29 - Columbus, OH, Ionian Room, Deshler-Wallick Hotel

30 - Canton, OH, Myer's Lake

31 - Mansfield, OH, Mansfield Theater; Leland Hotel

**February**

1 - open, Louisville, KY; Leland Hotel

2 - Hopkinsville, KY

3-9 - St. Louis, MO, St. Louis Theater; Melbourne Hotel

10 - Jackson, TN, Armory Pit; New Southern Hotel (mileage 280)

11-12 - Starkville, MS, Mississippi State University; Gilder Hotel
        (Columbus, OH)

13 - open

14 - Baton Rouge, LA, Harding Gym; Heidelberg Hotel

15 - Mobile, AL, Auditorium (mileage 200)

16 - Pensacola, FL, Mustin Beach Club; San Carlos Hotel (mileage 50)

17 - Selma, AL, Armory; San Carlos Hotel (Pensacola) (mileage 150)

18-19 - Pensacola, FL, Naval Air Base; San Carlos Hotel (mileage 150)

20 - Pensacola, FL, Mustin Beach Club

21 - Montgomery, AL, Southern Club; Exchange Hotel (mileage 180)

22 - Macon, GA, Club Royale (mileage 180)

23 - Savannah, GA, Auditorium; Dempsey Hotel (mileage 180)

24 - Columbia, SC, Columbia Theater; Wade Hampton Hotel (mileage 250)

25-26 - Raleigh, NC, University of North Carolina; Carolina Hotel
        (mileage 250)

27-March 2 - lay off, NYC; Belvedere Hotel

**March**

3 - Atlas Transcription date, NYC

4 - New Haven, CT, Yale University (mileage 300)

5 - Pottstown, PA, Sunnybrook Ballroom

6 - Baltimore, MD, Armory; Sheraton Hotel

7-11 - Philadelphia, PA, Click Club; Sylvania Hotel

12 - Moosick, PA, Pocky Glen Park

13-14 - open

15 - Providence, RI, Arcadia Ballroom

16 - Boston, MA, Theater; Avery Hotel

17 - Kingston, NY

18 - Alfred, NY, Alfred University

19 - Jersey City, NJ, Armory

20 - Holyoke, MA, Valley Arena; Roger Smith Hotel

21 -April 16 - NYC, Pennsylvania Hotel; President Hotel

## April

17-May 1 - Cedar Grove, NJ, Meadowbrook Ballroom; President Hotel (NYC)

## May

2 - open

3 - NYC, Standard Transcription date

4 - NYC, Columbia Recording date

5 - Allentown, PA

6 - Bethlehem, PA, Leheigh University

7 - Hershey, PA, Hershey Park

8 - open, NYC

9 - Montreal, Canada, Danceland Ballroom; Laurentian Hotel

10 - Quebec City, Canada, Latour Arena

11 - Montreal, Canada, Danceland Ballroom

12 - Lewiston, ME, Arena; Avery Hotel (Boston)

13-14 - Salem, NH, Canobie Lake; Avery Hotel (Boston)

15-21 - Wrentham, MA, King Philip Ballroom; Stage Coach Inn

22 - open

23 - NYC, Nola's Studio, rehearsal; Forrest Hotel

24 - NYC, Columbia Recording date

25 - NYC, Standard Transcription date

26 - open

27 - June 2 - Virginia Beach, VA, Surf Club

## June

3-4 - Charlotte, NC, Charlotte Hotel; O. Henry Hotel (Greensboro)
    (mileage 365/90)

5 - Durham, NC, Carolina Theater (mileage 60)

6 - open, Petersburg, VA; Petersburg Hotel (mileage 165)

7 - Fayetteville, NC, Willon's Warehouse; Prince Charles Hotel (mileage 200)

8 - Charleston, SC, Folly Beach Pier; St. John Hotel (mileage 200)

9 - Hickory, NC, Hickory Hotel (mileage 315)

10 - Rocky Mount, NC, New Hicks Hotel (mileage 250)

11 - Wilmington, NC, Cape Fear Hotel (mileage 150)

12 - open, Roanoke, VA, Patrick Henry Hotel (mileage 310)

13 - Charlottesville, VA, University of Virginia; Patrick Henry Hotel, Roanoke (mileage 260)

14 - Roanoke, VA, Auditorium

15 - Harrisburg, PA, Harrisburger Hotel (mileage 300)

16 - Mahoney City, PA, Lakewood Park; hotel in Harrisburg (mileage 160)

17 - Cumberland, MD, hotel in Harrisburg (mileage 260)

18 - Pottstown, PA, Sunnybrook Ballroom; Abe Lincoln Hotel, Reading (mileage 95)

19 - Moosick, PA, Pocky Glen Park; Abe Lincoln Hotel, Reading (mileage 150)

20 - open for travel to NYC; President Hotel

21 - Riverhead, LI, Regula's Corner; President Hotel, NYC (mileage 125)

22 - Saranac Lake, NY (fly from La Guardia Field)

23 - Clairmont, NH (leave after job)

24 - Manchester, NH, Carousel Ballroom; Carpenter Hotel

25 - Old Orchard Beach, MA, Pier; Carpenter Hotel, Manchester

26 - Bristol, CT, Lake Compounce; leave after job for Bond Hotel, Hartford

27 - open for travel to Buffalo, NY; Statler Hotel (mileage 400)

28 - Crystal Beach, Canada; Statler Hotel, Buffalo (mileage 50)

29 - Uniontown, PA; leave after job (mileage 250)

30 - open, stay in Clarksburg, WV; Stonewall Jackson Hotel (mileage 100)

## July

1 - Clarksburg, WV; leave after job for Baltimore, MD

2 - Chesapeake, MD; Emerson Hotel, Baltimore

3 - Ephrata, PA; leave after job for Utica Hotel, Albany, NY (mileage 400)

4 - Ritchfield Springs (Rome),NY, Sylvan Beach (mileage 300)

5-11 - NYC; vacation

11 - NYC, Paramount Theater (rehearsal); President Hotel

12 - Philadelphia, PA, Tower Theater; leave for NYC

13 - August 2 - NYC, Paramount Theater

*(WHEW!!)*

# WHERE WE SLEPT
## (or tried to!)

# HEY, _THIS_ WAS A BAND!

| | |
|---|---|
| JIMMY DORSEY | Leader, alto sax and clarinet |
| JAMES "DOC" CLIFFORD | 1st alto sax, clarinet |
| GENE "EAGLE" BOCKEY | 2nd alto sax, clarinet |
| ARTIE "HUMPHREY" LYONS | 1st tenor sax, clarinet |
| PHIL CENICOLA | 2nd tenor sax, clarinet, flute |
| MIMI "'MAD SICILIAN" LA ROCCA | Baritone sax, clarinet, bass clarinet |
| DICK HOFFMAN | 1st trumpet |
| CHARLIE "LITTLE T" TEAGARDEN | 2nd trumpet |
| JOE GRAVES | 3rd trumpet |
| MAX GUSSACK/MAYNARD FERGUSON | 4th trumpet |
| GEORGE MASSO/AL LORRAINE | 1st trombone |
| BRAD GOWANS/CHUCK MAXON | 2nd trombone |
| HERB WINFIELD, JR. | 3rd trombone/assistant conductor |
| ALVIN WASLOHN | Piano/arranger |
| BILL "LOW LIFE" LOLATTE | Bass |
| RAY "MOTHER" BAUDUC | Drums |
| ALAN REUSS | Guitar (recording sessions, only) |
| LARRY NOBLE | Boy vocalist |
| HELEN LEE/CLARE "SHANTY" HOGAN | Girl vocalists |
| HOWARD GIBELING/NEAL HEFTI | Arrangers |
| GIL KOERNER | Road manager |
| LILA "OLD WORMS" KOERNER | Secretary |
| GIBBY SEABORN | Band boy |
| AL "MOUSE" ROMANO | Valet/bodyguard |
| CHARLIE MUCCI | Bus driver |
| GENERAL ARTISTS CORPORATION (GAC)<br>    CORK O'KEEFE/TOMMY ROCKWELL | Management |

# INDEX

(Editor's note: Since there are so many references to Jimmy Dorsey, San Diego, California and New York City within the text of this book, we have opted to delete these items from the index.)